Le Creuset

Elisa Vergne · David Rathgeber · Photos: Thomas Duval

Cookbook

Les Éditions Culinaires

Contents

The enameled cast-iron casserole

Principles of Cooking

There's not much new about cooking in a casserole or a Dutch oven. Contemporary cookware has replaced the old-fashioned Dutch oven, a heavy pot with hot embers placed above and below it, that was used until the early nineteenth century. That, along with a roaster, and a heavy soup pot inevitably conjure up visions of delicious fragrances wafting from dishes simmering on the stove but the cookware used needs to be especially adapted for this type of cooking. The pots and pans need a thick, heavy bottom so the food cooks evenly, without getting burnt, and it needs a tight-fitting lid to prevent steam escaping and letting the food dry out while baking.

Gentle, healthy cooking

Slow-cooked foods are a cornerstone of the cooking traditions of European workers and peasants. This type of cooking is rich and delicious if the foods are prepared correctly in suitable utensils. Gentle cooking ensures that hotspots are avoided, because when food is burned, it can produce potentially toxic chemicals.

One of the best materials for the such cooking, enameled cast iron, is an excellent heat conductor. It has nothing to fear from progress and modernity, since it can cope with all types of fuel—wood or coal, gas, electricity, halogen, or induction heating. Inside the pot, the temperature gradually rises and the heat is distributed uniformly. This slow and even cooking method preserves the nutritional values, flavors and fragrances of ingredients prepared in this way.

Boiling and steaming

Food with a high water content (vegetables, fruits, meats, and fish) release part of their water during cooking, causing valuable water-soluble vitamins and minerals to be lost. To reduce this loss to a minimum, it's a good idea to cook these foods in as little water as possible. This method, known as "conservative cooking" enables the cooking liquid to become saturated with these nutrients thus preserving them in the food. The same is true when the foods are moistened with stock or broth. Furthermore, if foods are quickly sautéed before stewing or baking, a crust is formed, preventing the escape of more nutrients. The cooking can then continue in the the minimum amount of liquid—water, broth, or wine.

A few easy-to-follow healthy cooking rules:

- Choose the finest ingredients, containing as little fat as possible. Remove any excess fat before cooking.
- Add a minimum of grease, and use oil rather than butter, lard, or pork fat, all of which are rich in saturated fatty acids.
- Drain any foods that are first fried or sautéed and discard any fat remaining in the pan.
- Use of herbs, flavorings, and spices extensively.
- Re-use the cooking liquid from meats and vegetables. Their micronutrients will have dissolved in the cooking liquid, making a flavorful base for a sauce. Degrease the liquid if necessary.

In Practice

Braising

Food is cooked in its own juices, with very little liquid added at the start. The Doufeu Oven has been designed to avoid the cook having to check the food during cooking, which would otherwise have to be an almost continuous process. Ice water or ice cubes placed in its concave lid causes steam to form inside the pot and fall back down on the food immediately. The "flavor buds", the tiny bumps that cover the inside of the oven lid, also favor a completely even condensation of the steam which falls back inside the pot, moistening the foods uniformly, making them more melting and delicious. The food thus cooks without a reduction of the liquid, it does not stick to the oven, and can be left to simmer almost without supervision.

Baking

Enameled cast-iron cookware can be used to start the cooking process on the stovetop, and the casserole can then be transferred to the oven to complete the cooking gently and evenly. Dutch ovens, casseroles, and terrines, with tight-fitting lids are ideal for long, slow cooking.

Be gentle with me

Don't try to rush things. First heat your Le Creuset cookware empty. If you heat it very strongly, you risk cracking the enamel. To ensure that the pot or pan is sufficiently hot, perform a simple test. Throw a drop of water into it, if it splutters and evaporates it's a sign that the temperature is right. You can now add a little fat or oil and leave it to heat, then sauté the foods on medium heat. When they have cooked to the color you want, add a little liquid and stir and scrape the bottom of the pot to dissolve the caramelized cooking juices which will form the basis for the sauce. For turning the food over and dissolving the cooking juices (known as deglazing) use a wooden or Le Creuset silicone spatula or spoon, (that can take 800°F/400°C heat!). Use gentle heat, then add the necessary liquid. Bring to a boil, cover, reduce the heat and simmer on the heat or transfer the pot to the oven to bake.

Traditional Stoneware

This new, elegant range of cookware can be taken straight from the microwave oven to the table and even from the freezer to the oven (475°F/260°C maximum).

But be aware, traditional stoneware cannot be placed over a direct heat source of any kind!

If you use it under the broiler, leave a gap of at least 2½ inches/ 6 cm between the heat of the broiler and top of the recipient.

Cook it the night before!

Our grandmothers knew the secret! Once reheated, slow-cooked dishes taste even better. So cook the dish the night before and leave the food in the pot. Refrigerate it overnight, then gently reheat it the next day. This offers the additional advantage of letting you easily remove surplus fat from the surface of the cooking liquid.

Treating enameled cast-iron cookware right.

Enamel is a non-reactive material. It prevents the formation of rust and its smooth surface does not react with acids in foods such as tomatoes, vinegar, lemon, etc. It is also easy to clean. It is not totally shock-resistant, however, and can be scratched by knives and other metal cooking utensils. Wash your enameled cookware only in hot water with dishwashing detergent. If food has stuck to it, simply soak the pot for a while or, if you are in a hurry, fill it with water and heat it.

Use moderation: An urban myth holds that if food sticks to enamel, the enamel will retain the "memory" of it! The reality? If the food sticks the next time, unfortunately, this is because the heat used on it was too high.

If, despite all the precautions you have taken, the enamel splits or cracks on your cookware, there is no risk to health because the only substance capable of migrating to the food is iron, an element that is non-toxic and in fact essential to the human organism.

Even the black Le Creuset, despite its rather rustic appearance, is enameled. So treat it the same way as you would brightly colored Le Creuset cookware.

Great shapes, bright colors... and fun!

With their innovative and amusing, bright, and warm colors, Le Creuset cookware contributes fun to both kitchen and table. That's a good reason for making use of the other major advantage of the cookware, by bringing the roaster, casserole, or Dutch oven straight to the table. The cast iron will keep the dish hot for around 40 minutes, so you won't get sauce congealing as it waits for your guests to ask for second helpings. Food that remains hot without having to be reheated—a real boon! Your sense of smell will also have a feast—what delicious fragrances emerge when you lift the lid!

Cast iron also manages the cold well: If you have refrigerated a dish like Greek-style mushrooms or iced soup, you can be sure Le Creuset will keep it ice-cold on the table, even on a hot summer's day. You can even add ice to a fruit salad served in the pot, the ice won't melt away.

Soups
and Appetizers

Produce: choices and advice

Soups and Appetizers

Pumpkin:
Buy a large slice of a big (9 to 12-pound) orange pumpkin. The flesh should be juicy and the color bright.

Chicken broth:
You can make your own or use bouillon cubes (1 per 2 cups boiling water) or instant powder (1 large tablespoon per 2 cups boiling water). Use low-sodium versions if you do not want them to taste too salty.

Cream:
Use light cream or whipping cream containing 25% to 30% fat, and keep it very cold. If you are going to whip it, put it in the freezer for 15 minutes before doing so.

Lentils:
Gray-green Puy lentils are best. This is one of the few pulses that does not require pre-soaking before cooking. Just rinse the lentils in a colander under a cold water faucet.

Canadian bacon:
Use very slightly smoked bacon that is as lean as possible. Remove the rind and the fat next to it before cooking.

Rabbit:
Use a young rabbit with very white fat.

Parsley:
Flat-leaved parsley is more aromatic than curly parsley which is usually reserved for the garnish. If you don't have fresh herbs, use frozen ones.

Sausage:
There is a recipe that calls for a pork sausage called *sabodet* from the Lyons region. Other boiling sausages such as Kielbasa can be used instead, try and find ones containing pistachios.

Foie gras:
Duck foie gras has a stronger flavor than goose foie gras. Choose a firm piece that is pale beige in color, unblemished and with no traces of bitter gall. It should not be too large (around one pound). Soak it in iced water to which coarse salt has been added to firm it up. It will then be easier to work with.

Crawfish:
Choose large specimens for a gratin, with red claws if possible, as they have a better flavor. Avoid deep-frozen crawfish whose flesh has a tendency to be mealy.

Mignonnette pepper:
These are coarsely crushed peppercorns. If you can't find it, grind peppercorns in a peppermill set to the coarsest setting and used the more finely ground grains for another dish.

Eggs:
For casserole cooking, choose large, extra-fresh eggs weighing 3 ounces or more.

Chicken liver:
Buy pale chicken livers from the butcher as they have a better flavor. Carefully remove any trace of the bitter green gall. It is important to soak them for 15 minutes under cold running water.

Fish:
Fish fillets need to be as fresh as possible. If you cannot get perch or pike, you can also use tilapia, catfish, whitefish, or similar white-fleshed fish.

Le Comté cheese:
Your cheese soufflés will be more intensely flavored if you use this fruity, mature cheese from the Jura that is aged for at least 18 months. Specialty cheese shops know for how long their cheeses have been aged. Closest equivalent that is easier to find in the United States is any Swiss-type cheese such as Gruyère.

Pumpkin Soup
with chestnuts

Preparation time: 15 min.
Cooking time: 35 min.

To serve 4

2¼ lbs	pumpkin
1	onion
1	leek
2 cups	low-sodium chicken broth
2 tbsp	butter
1/3 cup	whipping cream, chilled
1 tbsp	olive oil
	salt and pepper

1. Discard the pumpkin seeds and fibers. Peel the pumpkin with a large knife and discard the skin. Cut the pulp into small pieces.

2. Peel the onion and cut it into thin strips. Trim the leeks and outer leaves of the leek, and cut off the hard green parts. Wash the leek and slice it into thin strips.

3. Heat the olive oil in a round Le Creuset pot. Add 4 teaspoons butter. Add the onion and leek and cook on gentle heat for 3 minutes.

4. Add the pieces of pumpkin to the pot, then the chicken broth. Bring to the boil and cover the pot. Simmer for 30 minutes.

5. Durée the contents of the pot in a food processor. Return to the heat and whisk in the rest of the butter. Check the seasoning.

6. Whip the cream and whisk it into the soup just before serving.

A contemporary note:
Serve the soup with 7 ounces of chestnuts (vacuum-packed) coarsely chopped for each diner to sprinkle over the soup.

Advice from the wine steward:
Accompany this soup with a white Pouilly-Fuissé.

Thick Lentil Soup
with Bacon

Preparation time: 10 min.
Cooking time: 45 min.

To serve 4

1 cup	Puy lentils
6 oz	slightly smoked lean bacon, in one piece
2	shallots
1	onion
1	carrot
2	garlic cloves
1	sprig of thyme
1	bayleaf
1	clove
	salt and pepper

1. Rinse the lentils under cold water and drain them. Peel the shallots, onion, carrot, and garlic. Chop the shallots. Stick the clove into the onion.

2. Put the lentils into a round Le Creuset pot. Add the bacon, shallots, onion, carrot, and garlic. Add 1 quart water. Bring to a boil and add the thyme and bayleaf. Cover and simmer for 40 minutes, skimming the surface 2 or 3 times. Ten minutes before the end of the cooking time, season with salt and pepper.

3. Remove the bacon, carrot, onion, thyme, bay leaf, and garlic. Pour the contents of the pot into a food processor and blend, or strain through a vegetable mill fitted with a fine screen. Strain through a fine sieve, then pour it back into the pot and reheat. Check and rectify the seasoning before serving.

A contemporary note:
This thick soup can be served with 3½ ounces/100 g foie gras, cooked and diced into ½-inch/1-cm cubes. These are distributed among the soup plates and the soup poured over them.

Advice from the wine steward:
Accompany this thick soup with a white Petit-Chablis.

Rabbit in Aspic
with Ravigote Sauce

Preparation time: 1 hr.
Cooking time: 1½ hrs.

To serve 6-8

1	3¼ lb/1.4 kg rabbit
	salt
2	carrots
2	onions
2	cloves
3	garlic cloves
3	sprigs flat-leaved parsley
2	sprigs savory
2 cups	dry white wine
8	bay leaf
10	white peppercorns
2 cups	dry white wine
2	chicken broth cubes
1 tbsp	Madeira jelly
	salt

1. Preheat the oven to 300°F. Cut the rabbit into serving pieces, (breaking the bones at the articulations so they do not break through the skin during cooking.) Season the pieces with salt. Reserve the liver and kidneys in the refrigerator.

2. Peel the carrots and slice them into rounds. Peel the onions and stick the cloves into them. Crush the garlic cloves. Rinse the parsley.

3. Put the rabbit into a Le Creuset oval soup pot. Add the onions, garlic, parsley, savory, bay leaf, and peppercorns. Pour in the white wine, then add just enough water to cover the rabbit. Add the soup cubes, cover the pot, and place it in the oven. Cook it for 90 minutes.

4. When the meat is very tender, drain it. Strain the liquid through a sieve lined with cheesecloth, and pour it back into the pot. Reduce it by half to 1 quart. Add the madeira jelly. Add the reserved liver and kidneys, and poach for 5 minutes, then remove and drain them. Leave the liquid to cool, then return it to the pot and reheat, stirring. Remove from the heat as soon as it comes to the boil, and leave to cool, refrigerating until the liquid jells.

5. Bone the rabbit and separate the flesh with a fork. Slice the liver and kidney into slices. Transfer all the rabbit pieces to a Le Creuset 1-quart rectangular terrine. Add the reduced cooking juices and Madeira jelly. Place the terrine in the refrigerator and leave it for the aspic to solidify for 24 hours.

A contemporary note:
Serve this rabbit terrine with a Ravigote Sauce. Crush a hard-cooked egg yolk with a teaspoon Dijon mustard and salt. Dissolve it in 3 tablespoons of wine vinegar, 5 tablespoons peanut oil, and 2 tablespoons olive oil. Mash the hard-cooked egg white with a fork, and add a few chopped cornichons, a few leaves of chopped chervil, flat-leaved parsley, and tarragon.

Advice from the wine steward:
Accompany the Rabbit in Aspic with a red Anjou-Villages.

Sabodet Sausage
in Wine

Preparation time: 20 min.
Cooking time: 40 min.

To serve 4

1 quart	Red Beaujolais
2	onions
2	cloves
1	sprig thyme
1	bay leaf
4	black peppercorns
1	sabodet, kielbasa or similar sausage (about 1 1/4 pounds weight)
8	small leeks
2 tbsp	vinaigrette dressing
1 tsp	butter
	salt and pepper

1. Pierce the sausage skin all over with a trussing-needle. Peel the onions and stick the cloves in them.

2. Pour the red wine into a Le Creuset oval soup pot. Add the onions, thyme, bay leaf, and peppercorns. Bring to the boil.

3. When the wine is boiling, add the sabodet sausage, reduce the heat, cover the pot and simmer so the liquid moves slightly for 30 minutes.

4. Trim the roots and hard green parts of the leeks. Split them down the center, wash them, and cook them for 20 minutes in salted boiling water. Drain them carefully. Place them in a Le Creuset oval dish and sprinkle them with the vinaigrette dressing.

5. Drain the sabodet sausage. Strain half the cooking liquid and reduce it until it has a syrupy consistency. Add the butter, beating constantly.

6. Remove the strings from around the sausage and slice it diagonally. Arrange the slices at one end of the dish, coat with sauce, sprinkle with pepper and serve hot.

If you cannot find sabodet sausage, make this dish with cervelas sausage containing pistachios, or kielbasa.

A contemporary note:
Garnish the leeks with some mini-croutons (¼ inch square) fried in butter.

Advice from the wine steward:
Accompany the sausage with a Red Saint-Amour.

Foie gras
in a Terrine

Soaking time:	3 hrs.	Cooking time:	40 min.
Preparation time:	40 min.	Resting time:	24 hrs.
Marinating time:	18 hrs.		+ 3-4 days

To serve 8

2	fresh duck foies gras weighing about 1 pound each
2 tsp	table salt
½ tbsp	freshly ground black pepper
⅓ cup	cognac
	coarse salt

A contemporary note:

Quince paste is a delicious accompaniment to this terrine. Peel 2 quinces, and cook them for 40 minutes in 1 quart water with a scant cup of sugar, and the rind and juice of 2 oranges. When they're cooked through, drain them and cut out the cores. Melt 2 tablespoons sugar in a dry saucepan until it starts to color, to make a caramel. Add the quince pieces and cook for 30 to 40 minutes, until the quinces turn pink and the cooking liquid is syrupy. You may need to add some of the cooking liquid from the first boiling of the quinces.

Advice from the wine steward:

Accompany the foie gras with a spicy white wine, Gewurztraminer from Alsace.

1. Separate the two lobes of the liver by hand. Scrape off any bitter green. Place the lobes in 2 quarts iced water with a large pinch of coarse salt. Soak for three hours.

2. Remove the livers from the water and pat them dry delicately. Remove the transparent membrane enclosing each lobe. Cut through each lobe with a small pointed knife to remove the main vein, starting from the thickest extremity. Pierce the flesh gently and gradually pull the vein free from underneath, using the knife. This main vein should draw the smaller veins out with it. Remove all traces of blood. Rinse the livers under cold running water and pat them dry with absorbent paper.

3. Drain the lobes on parchment paper. Combine the table salt and pepper and season the lobes of liver; sprinkle them with the cognac. Place them on top of each other in a small Le Creuset round French oven, pressing them down lightly. Add any liquids remaining drained on the nonstick baking paper. Cover the pot with plastic wrap and leave in the refrigerator to marinate until the next day.

4. Remove the French oven from the refrigerator and leave at room temperature for 30 minutes.

5. Preheat the oven to 210°F/100°C. Remove the plastic wrap from the pot and cover it with its lid. Place it in roasting pan and pour water into the pan halfway up the sides. Bring to the boil on the stovetop, then put the pan with the pot inside it into the oven. Cook for about 30 minutes, or until the center of the foie gras lobes reaches a temperature of 106°F/50°C. Remove the French oven from its water-bath and leave it to rest for 2 hours at room temperature.

6. Carefully drain the foies gras, pouring the fat into a small saucepan. Place a board or flat plate on the livers, and top it with a heavy weight (around 8 ounces) to press them flat. Refrigerate for 24 hours. Store the fat in the refrigerator.

7. The following day, remove the fat from the saucepan and discard any liquids in the pan. Melt the fat. When it stops spluttering, skim it and sleve it into a bowl placed on ice.

8. Remove the weight and the board from the French oven and smooth the top of the foie gras with a stainless steel spatula. Pour the fat which should be cold but liquid over the liver to preserve it from the air. Cover it again with a lid. Store the French oven in the refrigerator. The foie gras will be ready to eat in 3 or 4 days.

Slice the foie gras with a knife dipped in hot water and sprinkle each slice with sea salt and freshly ground black pepper.

Crawfish

Gratin

Preparation
and Cooking time: **40 min.**
Infusion: **15 min.**

To serve 4

24	large crawfish
3	garlic cloves
4	sprigs flat-leaved parsley
2 tbsp	oil
2 tbsp	cognac
	salt and pepper
1¼ cups	dry white wine (such as Aligoté Burgundy)
½ tsp	mignonnette pepper
⅓ cup	very cold whipping cream
4	egg yolks
6 tbsp	butter + more to grease the pans
½	lemon, juice squeezed

1. Wash the crawfish and twist the central part of the tail fin, pulling it off and taking the black vein with it. Detach the heads from the tails. Crush the garlic cloves without peeling them. Wash the parsley, pat it dry, and chop it.

2. Heat 1 tablespoon oil in a Le Creuset saucepan. Sauté the crawfish tails on high heat for 2 minutes. Remove the pot from the heat, add the garlic cloves and parsley. Cover with a damp cloth and leave to infuse for 15 minutes.

3. Remove the crawfish tails and empty the saucepan. Heat 1 tablespoon oil and sauté the tails again on high heat until they are very firm. Add the cognac and set it alight. When the flames are extinguished, scrape the bottom of the pot with a wooden spatula to dissolve the juices. Season with salt and generously with pepper. Cover the pot and remove from the heat.

4. Make a sabayon by reducing the white wine with the mignonnette pepper until it becomes syrupy. Remove it from the heat. Whip the cream. Add the egg yolks to the reduced white wine. Season with salt and beat the mixture in a bowl over a saucepan containing simmering water until the mixture thickens. Melt the butter and add it in twice, beating well after each addition. Then add the lemon juice and whipped cream, stirring without beating.

5. Lightly butter 4 Le Creuset individual gratin dishes. Divide the crawfish and their cooking juices between the dishes and coat them with the sabayon custard. Slide dishes under the broiler and broil for a few minutes, watching to ensure the custard does not burn.

You can also make this dish with shelled crawfish. Sauté them in butter with the garlic, deglaze with the cognac, cover and leave to infuse off the heat for 5 to 10 minutes. Then season generously with salt and pepper. Then all you have to do is make the sabayon custard.

Advice from the wine steward:
Accompany this gratin with a white wine such as Puligny-Montrachet.

Coddled Eggs
with Crawfish
and Garlicky Soldiers

Preparation
and cooking time: 20 min.

To serve 4

4	sprigs savory
⅓ cup	light cream
	salt and pepper
4	garlic cloves
2 tbsp	olive oil
⅓ cup	butter
3 cups	fresh spinach
8	cooked, peeled crawfish
4	eggs
2	small French baguette

1. Wash the savory and drain it. Finely chop the leaves. Pour the cream into a saucepan, add the savory and reduce the cream on low heat. When it has slightly thickened, season it with salt and pepper and keep it warm in a double boiler or bain-marie.

2. Peel 2 garlic cloves and add them to a small saucepan with the olive oil. Cook for around 15 minutes on low heat until they are soft but not melted. Drain them and cut them into little strips.

3. Heat the oven to 425°F/210°C. Prepare a water-bath by adding water to a roasting pan.

4. Sort, trim and wash the spinach. Peel one garlic clove and place it on the tines of a fork. Heat the butter in a Le Creuset saucepan until it turns pale brown. Then add the spinach and wilt it over medium heat, stirring with the fork on which the garlic clove has been stuck. Remove from the heat as soon as the spinach is cooked.

5. Divide the spinach between 4 Le Creuset mini-cocottes. Add the crawfish and a few strips of cooked garlic. Break 1 egg into each cocotte and cover it with the lid. Cook in the water-bath in the preheated oven for 10 minutes.

6. Slice the French baguette in half and broil them. Peel 1 garlic clove and cut it in two. Rub it lightly over the bread.

7. When the eggs are cooked, cover them with the savory cream, letting the yolks show through. Season with salt and one turn on the pepper mill. Place the cocottes on plates and serve with the French stick soldiers.

A contemporary note:
You could add wild mushrooms to these eggs in cocotte. Clean around 7 ounces of Horn of Plenty mushrooms and sauté them in butter with 1 garlic clove for 5 minutes. Season with salt and add ⅓ cup light cream. Cover and leave to infuse for 15 minutes off the heat. Drain the mushrooms, arrange them on top of the crawfish and add the garlic strips and then the egg. Bake in the oven. Combine the cooking liquids from the crawfish and from the mushrooms in a blender. Pour it over the eggs.

Advice from the wine steward:
Accompany these eggs in cocotte with a white wine such as a Condrieu.

Chicken Liver
Terrine

Preparation time:	30 min.	Cooking time:	75 min.
Resting time:	1 hr.	Refrigeration:	48 hrs.

To serve 6-8

1 lb 2 oz	chicken livers
1	caul fat
⅓ cup	cognac
	salt and pepper
14 oz	pork collar
½ tsp	mixed spice
2	sprigs fresh thyme
1	shallot
2	garlic cloves
1	egg

Advice from the wine steward:

Accompany this terrine with a white wine such as a Savennières.

1. Clean the chicken livers, discarding any greenish parts. Put them into a colander and place for 15 minutes under cold running water. Drain them, pat them dry and remove any connective tissue. Soak the caul in cold water.

2. Slice 3½ ounces of the chicken livers. Sprinkle with 2 tablespoons cognac, season lightly with salt and pepper, and leave to marinate.

3. Slice the pork collar into cubes, and grind it in a grinder with a fine mesh along with 14 ounces of the chicken livers. Stir the mixture well, adding 1 tablespoon, salt, 1 teaspoon pepper, the mixed spice, and the thyme leaves. Peel the shallot and garlic and chop them finely. Add them to the mixture, as well as the whole egg. Mix well and incorporate 5 tablespoons of the cognac.

4. Drain the caul fat and use it to line a Le Creuset 1-quart terrine, so that it also falls over the edge of the terrine. Arrange one third of the stuffing in the terrine, then cover with half the slices of liver, half the rest of the stuffing, and the rest of the liver slices, then the rest of the stuffing. Smooth the surface. Cover it with the excess caul, trimming any surplus to ensure it is evenly arranged. Press down well to remove any air pockets. Cover the terrine and refrigerate it for 1 hour.

5. Heat the oven to 350°F/170°C. Prepare a water-bath by pouring hot water into a large roasting pan. Place the covered terrine into the water-bath, the water should be hot but not boiling. Place in the oven and reduce the temperature to 300°F/150°C. Bake for 75 minutes.

6. Remove from the oven, remove the lid and let the terrine rest for 15 minutes. Then cover it with a wooden board, topped with a 7-ounce weight. Leave to cool at room temperature. Keep the covered terrine in the refrigerator for 48 hours before serving it with slices of toast.

A contemporary note:

Serve the terrine with mushrooms in vinegar. Peel and wash 2 cups button mushrooms, shiitake, or horn of plenty wild mushrooms. Drain them and macerate them in 1 tablespoon coarse salt for 1 hour. Then put the mushrooms into a pot with a few tarragon leaves sprinkled evenly around them. Boil ⅓ cup white wine vinegar with two peeled garlic cloves, ½ small chili pepper, ½ teaspoon coriander seeds, ½ teaspoon white peppercorns, and ½ teaspoon black peppercorns. Cover with the mushrooms. Leave to cool. Cover the pot and leave to marinate for 48 hours. This condiment can be kept in the refrigerator for 2 weeks in a hermetically sealed preserving jar.

Savory Cake with Olives
and Ham

Preparation time: 20 min.
Cooking time: around 45 min.

To serve 6-8

7 ounces	Smithfield ham
3 tbsp	black Greek-style olives
2 cups	all-purpose flour
1 tsp	baking powder
3	large eggs
⅓ cup	olive oil
⅓ cup	milk
6 tbsp	grated Gruyère cheese
1 tsp	chopped thyme
	cayenne pepper
	salt and pepper
	butter for the oven dish

1. Remove the skin and fat from the ham. Slice it into strips then dice it.

2. Cut the olives open from top to bottom, and remove the pit.

3. Heat the oven to 375°F/190°C. Butter a Le Creuset cake pan.

4. Combine the flour and baking powder and sift them into a bowl. Make a well in the center. Break the eggs into a small bowl and beat them with a fork. Season them with salt and pepper then add a pinch of cayenne pepper and the thyme. Add the eggs, oil, and milk to the well in the center of the flour mixture, then stir with a wooden spoon, gradually incorporating the flour.

5. When the batter is smooth, add the diced ham, olive pieces and grated Gruyère cheese. Pour the batter into the cake pan. Smooth the surface with a damp spatula.

6. Put the cake into the oven and bake for around 45 minutes, or until a metal skewer inserted into the center comes out dry. Remove the cake from the oven and leave it to rest for 15 minutes before unmolding it. Let it rest on a cake rack.

Terrine of Fish,
with Tomato Sauce

Preparation time: **30 min.** Cooking time: **75 min.**
Refrigeration time: **2 hrs.** Resting time: **24 hrs.**

To serve 6

1¼ lbs	perch, pike, or carp flesh
2	shallots
2 tsp	butter + more for the terrine
4	sprigs flat-leaved parsley
3	sprigs tarragon
4	sprigs chervil
	salt and pepper
1	egg
1 cup	light cream
1/3 cup	heavy cream

1. Rinse the fish, pat it dry, cut it into pieces and grind it in a grinder with a small holes. Do this twice more. Chill the ground fish in the refrigerator for 2 hours.

2. Peel the shallots and mince them. Melt 2 teaspoons butter in a skillet and add the shallots. Cook them but do not let them color. Leave them to cool.

3. Rinse the herbs, pat them dry, pull off the leaves, and chop them finely.

4. Place the ground fish in the chilled bowl of a food processor*. Season with salt and pepper. Add the egg and process for around 10 seconds so that the mixture is smooth. Incorporate the light cream and the heavy cream. Do not process for too long, to prevent the ground fish from getting too warm.

5. Remove three-fifths of the ground fish and refrigerate it. Incorporate the rest of the cooked shallots and the herbs. Refrigerate the mixture.

6. Heat the oven to 275°F/140°C. Make a water-bath by pouring water into a roasting pan. Lightly butter a Le Creuset 1-quart rectangular terrine. Put one-third of the ground fish mixture into the terrine, cover it with half the herbed fish, continue with half of the rest of the ground fish, the rest of the herbed fish, and complete with the rest of the ground fish. Cover the terrine with its lid. Put it in the water-bath, place it in the oven, and bake for 75 minutes.

7. Check for doneness by pushing a trussing needle into the center of the mixture and bring it to your lips; it should be hot. Remove the terrine from the water-bath, leave to cool at room temperature, then chill for 24 hours in the refrigerator.

*To chill the food-processor bowl, refrigerate it for at least15 minutes before use.

Contemporary note:
Prepare a tomato sauce to accompany the terrine. In a small Le Creuset saucepan heat 2 tablespons olive oil and gently cook 1 onion peeled with green shoot removed and coarsely chopped, 2 garlic cloves cut in half and green shoot removed. Skin 4 tomatoes, quarter them, and deseed them. Leave them to drain for a few minutes, then season them with 1 teaspoon colombo spice blend, 1 sprig of thyme and ½ bayleaf. Season with salt, then cover and b ake in the oven at 210°F/100°C for 30 minutes. Mix well, season with 2 drops of Tabasco, and leave to cool.

Advice from the wine steward:
Accompany the terrine with a Lirac white wine.

Soufflé

with Vieux Comté Cheese

| Preparation: | 15 min. |
| Cooking time: | 20 min. |

To serve 6

1½ oz	Vieux Comté cheese
4	small eggs
2 tbsp	butter
2 tbsp	all-purpose flour
1 cup	milk
dash	salt
dash	nutmeg
a little	very soft butter for greasing the ramekins

1. Preheat the oven to 425°F/220 °C. Finely grate the cheese. Separate the egg whites from the yolks.

2. Heat the butter in a saucepan. Add the flour and mix with a wooden spatula for 1 minute, without letting the mixture color. Gradually add the milk, stirring constantly with a hand-whisk. Bring to the boil, still stirring, then cook this Béchamel sauce on a low heat for 2 minutes. Season with salt and add 1 pinch nutmeg.

3. Remove the mixture from the heat and incorporate the Vieux Comté cheese. Then add the egg yolks.

4. Add 1 pinch of salt to the egg whites and beat them into stiff peaks with an electric beater. Add a quarter of the whites to the mixture to soften it, beating well. Fold in the rest of the whites.

5. Carefully butter 6 Le Creuset ramekins that hold just under one cup. Use a pastry brush and ensure that the ramekins are buttered right to the top. Fill them to within ½ inch of the edge. Smooth with a spatula. Bake, then reduce the temperature to 400°F/200°C and cook for a further 12 minutes, without opening the oven door during the cooking time. Serve immediately.

Advice from the wine steward:
Accompagny this soufflé with a white wine such as Côtes-du-Jura.

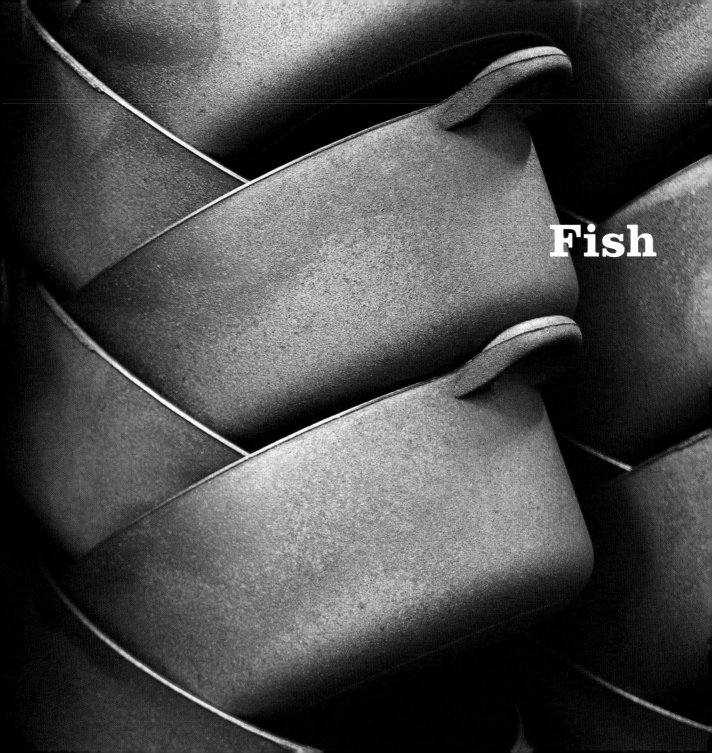

Fish

Produce: choices and advice

Fish

Monkfish:
This firm-fleshed fish is native to the Atlantic and Mediterranean; it is also known as the anglerfish. If it is not available, use redfish, pollock, or other firm-fleshed white fish. Remove all of the monkish skins (there are seven of them!) before cooking, as leaving them on will make the fish rubbery.

Garlic:
Whether white, pink, or red, garlic is used as the basis for the garlic sauce known as aïoli. Use fresh, white garlic in spring. In winter, choose pink garlic, French Lautrec garlic benefits from an AOC (appellation d'origine contrôlée). Except in spring, always cut the cloves in half and remove the small green shoot which many people find indigestible.

Fish fumet or broth:
You can make a fish fumet or broth yourself, using fish trimmings (heads and bones) of white fish or use a powdered fish broth. Be aware that the powder has a high salt content.

Olive oil:
Essential in an aïoli, but olive oil needs to correspond to your tastes. Always use extra-virgin oil with a regulation acidity of less than 1%. Avoid oils that are too fruity if you are not used to them.

Eel:
In France, eel is found in the Rhône river and its tributaries mainly in fall and winter. Eel can be ordered from a fishmonger who will skin it for you.

Bacon and salt pork:
Use salt pork belly for casserole cooking. It needs to be blanched first (put it in a saucepan of cold water, bring to the boil and rinse under cold water) to remove the salt.

Pearl onions:
These small, dry, yellow-skinned onions are only around 1 inch in diameter.

Mushrooms:
It is best to use very white button mushrooms with closed caps, and leave them whole. You can also slice larger mushrooms into quarters.

Brill:
This delicately flavored flatfish is found in the Mediterranean. Other flatfish such as halibut, turbot, or sole can be substituted. It needs to be cooked in a large flat dish big enough to take the whole fish but it can also be cooked as filets or steaks. The skin should be very shiny.

Caul fat:
This fine, lacy membrane of pork fat can be ordered from a pork-butcher. Rinse it carefully in cold water and leave it to soak, to release any impurities. Be careful in handling it, so you do not tear it.

Frogs:
Only the legs, or rather the thighs, of this amphibian are eaten. They are usually sold threaded on wooden skewers. You just need to remove the skewer, leaving the legs in pairs.

Flat-leaf parsley and chervil:
Chop these herbs on a board using a very sharp knife so as not to crush them or cause them to blacken. Always chop herbs at the last minute to prevent them from losing their fragrance and flavor.

Bourride

Sétoise

Preparation time: 20 min.
Cooking time: 40 min.

To serve 4

2 lb 12 oz	monkfish
2	small leeks, whites only
1	onion
2	small carrots
1	tomato
3	sprigs flat-leaf parsley
2	garlic cloves
4 tbsp	olive oil
1 cup	fish fumet
	salt and pepper
1 cup	dry white wine
	For the Aïoli
4	garlic cloves
	salt
1	egg yolk
2 tbsp	olive oil

1. Skin the fish. Cut the fish into thick slices, leaving the backbone in place.

2. Trim the roots and discard the first skin of the white parts of the leeks. Wash the leeks and slice them thinly. Peel the onion and slice it into rings. Peel and dice the carrots. Wash the tomato and chop it coarsely. Rinse the parsley. Peel and chop the garlic.

3. Pour 2 tablespoons olive oil into a Le Creuset pot and add the leeks, onion, carrots and tomato. Simmer the vegetables for 5 minutes. Add the parsley, garlic, and fish fumet. Mix well, and season lightly with salt and with pepper. Cover the saucepan, bring it to the boil on low heat, and simmer for 15 minutes, stirring from time to time. Then add the wine and simmer for 10 minutes.

4. Season the monkfish. Heat 2 tablespoons olive oil in a sauté pan, and cook the monkfish slices until they turn color, about 1 minute on each side. Reduce the heat and simmer on low heat for 2 minutes on each side. Drain the fish on a rack over a dish.

5. Filter the contents of the saucepan, recovering the cooking liquid. Pour it back into the saucepan and add the liquid from the fish. Return the saucepan to the heat and place the fish in the liquid. Cover and simmer on low heat for 10 to 15 minutes, depending on the thickness of the fish.

6. To make the Aïoli, peel the garlic cloves, cut them in half and remove the green shoot in the center. Crush the garlic in a mortar with a pinch of salt. Add the egg yolk, and continue grinding for 2 minutes with the pestle. Gradually incorporate the olive oil, drop by drop, continuing to grind with the pestle always in the same direction.

7. Heat a Le Creuset oval ovenproof dish. Drain the monkfish and arrange it in the heated dish. Cover it. Reduce the cooking liquid in a saucepan until you have around 1¼ cups. Check the seasoning. Add the aïoli, beating constantly with a hand whisk. Coat the fish with the sauce and serve immediately.

A contemporary note:
Garnish the monkfish slices with croûtons sautéed in butter and spread with a little of the aïoli sauce.

Advice from the wine steward:
Accompany this fish stew with a white wine such as a Coteaux-du-Languedoc.

Eel Slices
in Matelote Sauce

Preparation
and Cooking time: 40 min.

To serve 4

2	onions
1	carrot
1	celery stick
1	garlic clove
2 1/4 lb	skinned eel
½ cup	butter
3 tbsp	Marc de Bourgogne
1	bouquet garni
1	clove
5	peppercorns
1 quart	dry red wine
20	pearl onions
1 tsp	sugar
2 cups	mushrooms
6 oz	salt pork belly
	salt

1. Peel the 2 onions and the carrot. Remove the strings from the celery stick, and slice the vegetables into small strips. Peel and crush the garlic.

2. Slice the eel. Heat 3½ tablespoons butter in a Le Creuset pot. Sauté the slices of eel until the flesh is firm. Add the Marc de Bourgogne and set it alight.

3. Add the sliced vegetables, garlic, bouquet garni, clove, and peppercorns. Season with salt and add the red wine. Bring to the boil, then reduce the heat and simmer gently, uncovered, for 20 minutes.

4. Peel the pearl onions. Put them into a small saucepan with 4 teaspoons butter, the sugar, and 5 tablespoons water. Place a round of nonstick baking paper over the onions and cook on low heat for 10 minutes. Coat the onions in their cooking liquid.

5. Trim the mushroom stalks and sauté the mushroom in 1 tablespoon butter. Season with salt.

6. Cut the salt pork into short strips. Put them in a saucepan of cold water, drain them, and bring to the boil. Rinse under cold running water. Then add 2 teaspoons butter to a skillet and sauté them on low heat.

7. When the eel is cooked, drain it. Filter the cooking liquid and reduce it by two-thirds. Check the seasoning. Put the fish into the sauce with the mushrooms and simmer for 5 minutes. Add the onions and salt pork. Serve very hot from the pan.

A contemporary note:
Accompany the dish with little croûtons fried in butter.

Advice from the wine steward:
Serve the eel with a white wine such as a Sancerre.

Braised Brill
in Champagne

Preparation time: **40 min.**
Cooking time: **1 hr.10 min.**

To serve 4

1	brill, weighing 3½ lb gutted
7 oz	button mushrooms
8	shallots
4	garlic cloves
⅔ cup	butter
1	sprig of flat-leaf parsley
8	peppercorns
1	carrot
1	bottle of champagne
4	egg yolks
	salt
	lemon juice
½	lemon

1. Rinse the brill under cold running water. Remove the head, and trim the barbs, reserving them. Slice the fish into 4 equal-sized pieces.

2. Trim the mushroom stalks. Wash the mushrooms and slice them vertically. Peel the shallots and slice them. Peel the garlic and remove the green shoot in the center. Crush the garlic.

3. Melt 2 tablespoons butter in a Le Creuset saucepan and add the fish. Cook on low heat for 3 minutes. Add half the mushrooms, half the garlic, and half the shallots. Continue to cook for 2 minutes. Add 2½ cups of the champagne and simmer gently for 45 minutes.

4. Remove the pot from the heat. Rinse the parsley, and add it with 5 peppercorns. Cover and leave to infuse for 20 minutes. Filter this base for the sauce.

5. Heat the oven to 350°F. Peel the carrot and slice it at an angle into rings ⅛ inch thick.

6. Melt 3½ tablespoons butter in a Le Creuset oval ovenproof dish. When the butter is foaming, add the carrot, 3 peppercorns, the rest of the mushrooms, the garlic, and shallots. Cook for 5 minutes. Add ⅓ cup champagne and stir the dish well with a wooden spatula to dislodge anything sticking to the sides and bottom. Arrange the fish slices in the ovenproof dish, cover with nonstick baking paper, and bake for 15 to 18 minutes.

7. Pour the base for the sauce into a saucepan. Add the egg yolks and ¾ cup champagne. Beat with a whisk over low heat until the sauce thickens slightly, without letting it boil. Cut the rest of the butter into small pieces and beat them in, whisking well after each addition. Rectify the seasoning. Add a little lemon juice to flavor the sauce and then add the rest of the champagne.

8. Drain the slices of brill and remove the dark skin. Clean the ovenproof dish and return the fish to it. Coat them with a little of champagne sauce, and pour the rest of the sauce into a warmed sauceboat to serve.

A contemporary note:
Garnish the dish with a few skinned, boiled pearl onions.

Advice from the wine steward:
Serve the brill with a Blanc-de-Blancs champagne.

Monkfish Fillets
with Basil

Preparation time: 15 min.
Cooking time: 15 min.

To serve 4

1	caul fat
2¼ lb	monkfish
3-4	sprigs of basil
	salt and pepper
3 tbsp	olive oil
⅓ cup	chicken broth
2 tsp	butter

1. Soak the caul fat in a bowl of cold water. Preheat the oven to 400°F.

2. Cut the fish away from the backbone lengthwise, using a sole filleting knife. Carefully remove all the skins.

3. Wash the basil and remove the leaves. Plunge the leaves into cold water, bring to the boil, then refresh the leaves in cold water. Pat them dry carefully.

4. Drain the caul and spread it out carefully on the work surface. Cut it in half. Arrange the basil leaves side-by-side on each piece of caul fat, ensuring the are the same length as the fish fillets. Place a monkfish fillet on top of the basil. Season with salt and pepper and roll them up in the caul fat. Tie with string, but do not tie too tightly.

5. Heat 2 tablespoons olive oil in an oval Le Creuset ovenproof dish. Sauté the fish fillets for 2 minutes on each side, then slide the ovenproof dish into the oven and bake for 15 minutes.

6. Remove the fish fillets from the oven, remove them from the dish and keep them warm. Pour ⅓ cup chicken broth into the cooking dish, over low heat, stirring with a spatula to dislodge any pieces that have stuck to the bottom. Cut 2 teaspoons butter into little pieces, and add them piece by piece, beating well with a whisk after each addition. Then add 2 teaspoons olive oil, gently shaking the dish over the heat.

7. Slice the fish pieces, transfer them to the ovenproof dish, and coat with a little of the sauce.

A contemporary note:
Make small cuts in the monkfish at regular intervals and insert pieces of sundried tomato in them. Surround with pitted black olives.

Advice from the wine steward:
Accompany the monkfish with a white wine such as a Pernand-Vergelesses.

Frogs' Legs
with Parsley and Chervil

Preparation
and Cooking time: 20 min.

To serve 4

1	small bunch flat-leaf parsley
1	small bunch chervil
2	garlic cloves
1	lemon
⅛ cup	softened butter
⅔ cup	all-purpose flour
	salt and pepper
2 tbsp	oil
3	dozen frogs' legs

1. Rinse the parsley and chervil and pat them dry. Remove the leaves and mince them. You should have 3 tablespoons of each herb. Peel the garlic and remove the sprout inside the cloves. Squeeze them in a garlic press. Squeeze the 1/2 lemon. Combine the softened butter, parsley, chervil, garlic and lemon juice in the bowl of a food process. Season with salt and pepper and process until smooth.

3. Pour the flour into a shallow bowl. If the frogs' legs have been threaded on skewers, remove them and discard the skewers. Season them with salt and pepper and coat them in the flour. Shake them in a fine sieve to remove any excess flour.

4. Heat the oil in a Le Creuset oval ovenproof dish. Add the frogs' legs and sauté them on high heat for 4 minutes.

5. Squeeze 1/2 lemon. Reduce the heat under the frogs' legs, pour the lemon juice into the dish and scrape the bottom of the recipient with a wooden spatula. Add the parsley butter and heat until it foams, shaking the dish gently. Serve immediately.

Advice from the wine steward:
Serve the frogs' legs with a white wine such as a Chablis.

Meats

Produce: choices and advice
Meats

Lamb:
In France, lamb is the meat of a sheep aged less than 300 days. After that, it becomes mutton. The finest French lamb comes from Limousin, chosen for the size of the legs. Lamb meat should be pink, not bright red, and not too fatty. The fat should be pale. You may need to remove excess fat from the shoulder.

Beef:
Order a beef cheek from the butcher (a cheek weighs about 1 pound 5 ounces).
Chuck, brisket, shank, and plate are all excellent, flavorful cuts that become very tender if cooked slowly on low heat. The longer the cooking time, the more meltingly delicious the meat. Try and cook the largest quantities possible, in order to spread the cooking time and especially because dishes will be better if they are reheated. To do this, cover the heat source with a heatproof mat to reduce the heat or cook them in an oven preheated to 325°F.

Citrus zest:
Use untreated fruits, scrub the skins in warm water, then pat them dry. Remove the zest in a long strip with a small, sharp knife, and with a citrus-zester to make julienne strips. You can also use a grater. Always make sure never to include the white parts as they are bitter.

Pork:
Salt pork belly or pancetta should not be too fat, it should have equal amounts of lean and fat. If it is too lean, it will be dry. Pork cheeks can be ordered from the butcher. Ham hocks are available from the butcher and, for this recipe, they should be boned. Ask your butcher to tell you how long you need to soak the pork in order to remove the salt.
Pork tenderloin should be very pale. It should not be larded, barded, or trussed.

Lentils:
See in page 10.

Cabbage:
Choose fully rounded, compact dark-green cabbages. Discard the outer leaves, wash the whole cabbage in water to which a few drops of vinegar have been added, holding it head down.

Celery sticks:
These may be used as the white part only, the leaves only, or the whole stick, including the leaves. Rinse them carefully and take time to remove the strings from the sticks.

Foie gras:
See page 10.

Duck fat:
Order it from the butcher or poultry dealer. Some supermarkets may sell it in jars.

Prunes:
Choose large soft fruits. You will save time if they are already pitted.

Veal:
The best veal-calves are raised alongside their mothers and fed with their milk. Their flesh is white with a fine, delicate flavor. If you cannot get milk-fed veal, the flesh should be pink and only slightly fatty.
To be assured of the finest meat taken from the hind leg (which is meatier), order a knuckle of veal from your butcher. Ask him not to trim it too finely, so that the bone does not become detached during cooking.
A veal blanquette is best if you use meat from various parts of the animal. The breast has the best flavor thanks to the bones, the shoulder is tender.

Chicken broth:
See page 10.

Beef broth:
You can make it yourself or use bouillon cubes (1 per 2 cups boiling water).

Spoon-soft or Seven-hour
Leg of Lamb

Preparation time: 15 min.
Cooking time: 7 hrs.

To serve 8

2	onions
2	carrots
1	head garlic
2 tbsp	oil
1	short leg of lamb (5 lb 8 oz)
5	thin slices smoked bacon
1	bay leaf
2	sprigs thyme
1 tbsp	tomato paste
⅓ cup	dry white wine
	salt and pepper

1. Peel and dice the onions and carrots. Crush the garlic cloves without peeling them.

2. Heat the oil in a Le Creuset oval French oven the right size for the length of the leg of lamb. On high heat, sauté the leg of lamb on all sides. Remove it and replace it with the onions and carrots. Sauté until the onion softens, then remove them.

3. Cover the bottom of the pot with slices of bacon and place the leg on top. Add the onions and carrots, bay leaf, thyme, and garlic cloves. Dissolve the tomato paste in the wine, and pour this into the pot, then add 1¼ cups water. Season with salt and pepper and bring to the boil.

4. Cover the pot. Reduce the heat and cook on a very low heat (the water should barely shiver) for seven hours.

5. Remove 2 cups of the cooking liquid. Strain it, degrease it, then reduce it by one-third over high heat. Carefully remove the leg of lamb from the pot and place it on a heating serving platter. Serve the leg of lamb with a spoon and pour the cooking liquid into a sauceboat to serve as gravy.

To obtain a nice, caramelized crust, place the pot in a preheated 275°F oven, and cook for 7 hours, basting every 30 minutes with its cooking juices.

Advice from the wine steward:
Accompany the lamb with a red wine, such as a Chambolle-Musigny.

Stewed Lamb
Provençal-style

Preparation time: **30 min.**
Cooking time: **2 hrs. 30 min.**

To serve 4

2¼ lb	shoulder of lamb
	salt and pepper
2	onions
2	carrots
2	tomatoes
4	garlic cloves
2 tbsp	olive oil
1 tbsp	tomato paste
1 cup	white wine
1	sprig of thyme
1	bay leaf
20	Greek black olives

1. Remove as much fat as possible from the meat. Cut the meat into pieces weighing around 3 ounces each. Season them with salt and pepper. Peel the onions and carrots, and dice them. Skin the tomatoes and cut them into quarters. Peel the garlic and crush the cloves.

2. Preheat the oven to 350°F. Heat the olive oil over the fire in a Le Creuset Doufeu pot. Sauté the pieces of meat, browning them all over on medium heat.

2. Remove the meat from the pot and replace it with the onions and carrots. Leave them to cook for a few minutes over low heat. Use a tablespoon to remove as much fat as possible from the pot. Add the tomato paste and mix well. Return the meat to the pot, add the white wine, and scrape the bottom of the bottom with a spatula to dislodge anything that has stuck to it.

3. Add the tomatoes, garlic, thyme, and bayleaf to the pot with 1¼ cups water. Season with salt and pepper and bring to the boil. Cover the Doufeu pot and pour ice water into the concave lid. Place the Doufeu in the oven and reduce the temperature to 325°F. Cook for two and a half hours, checking the contents of the pot and stirring from time to time.

4. Pit the olives. Add them 20 minutes before the end of the cooking time.

5. When the stew is cooked, remove the meat with a skimmer. Discard the thyme and bayleaf. Degrease the cooking liquid with a spoon, check the seasoning, then pour it over the meat.

Advice from the wine steward:
Accompany the stew with a strong red wine such as a Bandol.

Lamb
with Spring Vegetables

Preparation time: 40 min.
Cooking time: 90 min.

To serve 4

1	large onion
2	garlic cloves
2¼ lb	boned shoulder of lamb
	salt and pepper
2	tomatoes
2 tbsp	oil
1	bouquet garni
1 cup	white wine
8 oz	baby turnips
8 oz	baby carrots
1 lb	small waxy potatoes
4 oz	green beans
8	small onions
4 tsp	butter
1 tsp	sugar

1. Preheat the oven to 325°F. Peel the large onion and garlic, mince the onion and crush the garlic. Cut the meat into ½-inch cubes, and season with salt and pepper. Wash the tomatoes, skin them, peel them, and cut them into quarters.

2. Heat the oil in a Le Creuset Doufeu pot and brown the meat all over. Remove it with a skimmer. Replace it with the onion, garlic, and the bouquet garni. Cook on low heat for a few minutes.

3. Return the meat to the pot. Pour the white wine over it and scrape the bottom of the pot with a wooden spatula to dislodge any bits that have stuck to it. Add the tomatoes and around 1¼ cups hot water, enough to almost cover the meat. Season with salt and pepper. Bring to the boil slowly, then cover the pot, and fill the concave lid with ice water. Side the pot into the oven and cook for 90 minutes.

4. Meanwhile, peel the turnips, carrots, and potatoes, then wash them. Top and tail the green beans, break them into short lengths, and wash them. Put the potatoes into a saucepan of salted water and cook for 15 minutes. Cook the turnips and carrots for 10 minutes in boiling salted water. Cook the green beans for 8 minutes in boiling salted water. Drain and reserve all the vegetables as they have cooked.

5. Twenty minutes before the end of the cooking time for the meat, add the turnips, carrots, and potatoes to the Doufeu pot. Add the green beans 10 minutes later.

6. Peel the pearl onions and put them in a small pan with butter, sugar, and 4 tablespoons water. Cover with a disk of nonstick baking paper and cook until they are coated in a brown glaze. Add them to the pot 5 minutes before the meat has finished cooking.

Advice from the wine steward:
Accompany this spring lamb with a red wine such as Côtes-du-Rhône-Villages-Rasteau.

Beef Burgundy-style

Preparation time: **30 min.**
Marinating time: **24 hrs.**
Cooking time: **3 hrs.**

To serve 6

1	onion
2	shallots
3 lb 5 oz	braising beef (chuck, skirt, brisket) cut into 1-inch cubes
1	sprig of thyme
1	bay leaf
1 tsp	crushed peppercorns
1 quart	dry red wine
1 tbsp	oil
7 oz	smoked lean pork belly
2 tbsp	oil
6 tbsp	butter
2 tbsp	all-purpose flour
	salt and pepper
24	pearl onions
1 tsp	sugar
1	sprig of thyme
1	bayleaf

1. First make the marinade. Peel the onion and shallots and slice them thinly. Put the meat into a Le Creuset French oven or casserole, add the onion and shallots, thyme, bay leaf, and crushed peppercorns. Add the red wine and oil. Stir with a wooden spoon, then cover and leave in the refrigerator to marinate for 24 hours.

2. The next day, drain the meat, retaining the marinade. Pat the meat dry and strain the marinade. Cut the rind and cartilage from the pork belly and cut it into short strips. Bring the marinade to the boil.

3. Heat the oil in the Le Creuset pot and add half the butter. When the fat is hot, add the meat and pork belly and brown them all over for a few minutes. Remove them from the pot with a skimmer.

4. Discard the grease in the pot. Melt another 4 teaspoons butter, return the meat to the pot without the pork belly and sprinkle with the flour. Mix well on medium heat, turning the pieces of meat over from time to time. Add the hot marinade to the pot with the thyme and bay leaf. Season with salt and pepper and cook on very low heat, so the water barely shivers for 2 hours 45 minutes.

5. Peel the pearl onions and add them to a small saucepan with the rest of the butter, the sugar and 4 or 5 teaspoons of water. Cover with a disk of nonstick baking paper and simmer for around 10 minutes. Add 1 tablespoon of the meat cooking liquid and coat the onions in the glaze.

6. When the beef has been cooking for 2 hours 45 minutes, discard the thyme and bayleaf. Add the onions and reserved pork belly and cook for another 15 minutes, or until the meat is really tender. Serve very hot.

Don't forget that the cooking time is proportionate to the size of the pieces of meat. Check for doneness by piercing the meat with a knife point. It should sink into the meat without encountering any resistance.

Advice from the wine steward:
Accompany this beef stew with a red wine such as a Gevrey-Chambertin.

Beef Cheek
Casserole

Preparation time: **30 min.**
Marinating time: **24 hrs.**
Cooking time: **4 hrs.**

To serve 6

3	beef cheeks
	salt and pepper
1	carrot
2	onions
2	celery sticks
1 quart	strong red wine (such as Cahors)
1	small glass cognac
4 tbsp	olive oil
5	peppercorns
3	sprigs of flat-leaf parsley
2	sprigs of thyme
1	bay leaf
4	garlic cloves
1	cinnamon stick
3	cloves
1	strip orange peel
2	tomatoes

1. Put the beef cheeks into a bowl and season them with salt and pepper. Peel the carrot and onions and slice them into rounds. Remove the strings from the celery and slice it. Add the vegetables to the meat. Cover with red wine, add the cognac, 2 tablespoons olive oil, the peppercorns, parsley, thyme, and bay leaf. Cover and leave to marinate for 24 hours in the refrigerator.

2. The next day, preheat the oven to 325°F. Peel and crush the garlic, remove the green shoot in the center of the cloves, and slice them into 4.

3. Drain the meat, reserving the marinade. Pat the meat dry with kitchen paper. Heat 2 tablespoons of the olive oil in a Le Creuset Doufeu pot and sauté the meat all over on medium heat.

4. Filter the marinade. Add its solid ingredients to the pot, with the tomatoes and garlic. Simmer for a few minutes.

5. Heat the marinade, and pour it into the pot. Add the cinnamon stick, cloves, and piece of orange peel. Season with salt and pepper. Bring to the boil, and cover. Pour ice water into the concave lid of the Doufeu pot. Slide the pot into the oven and bake for at least 4 hours.

6. When the meat is tender, drain it and reserve it. Degrease the cooking liquid and strain it, then pour it back into the pot. Reduce it if it seems to be too watery. Return the meat to the pot, reheat it for a few minutes, and serve it very hot.

If the cooking liquid does not seem strong enough to serve as gravy, add half a tablespoon red wine vinegar to it.

If any of this dish is left over, serve it cold the next time with a well-flavored potato salad. You can also reheat it gently. Slow cooked stews taste even better when reheated.

Advice from the wine steward:
Accompany this stew with a red wines such as a Cornas.

Stewed Beef

Chuck or Brisket

Preparation time: **20 min.**
Cooking time: **around 6 hrs.**

To serve 6-8

4	large onions
4	carrots
2 tbsp	oil
3½ lb	chuck or brisket
1	bouquet garni
3	garlic cloves
1¾ cups	white wine
2 quarts	beef broth
2 tbsp	tomato paste
2 tbsp	all-purpose flour
	salt and pepper

1. Preheat the oven to 350°F. Peel the onions and chop them fairly finely. Peel the carrots, wash them, and cut them into rounds.

2. Heat the oil in a Le Creuset oval casserole and sauté the meat all over on medium heat. When it has turned color, remove it, and replace it with the onions, carrots, bouquet garni, and unpeeled garlic cloves. Cook for a few minutes on low heat.

3. Heat the white wine with the broth and tomato paste. Add the flour, beating with a hand-whisk to prevent the formation of lumps.

4. Return the meat to the casserole, cover it with the contents, and bring to the boil. Cover the casserole and put it in the oven. Bake it for around six hours , or until the meat is tender.

5. At the end of the cooking time, taste the cooking liquid. If it is not strongly flavored enough, pour it into a saucepan to reduce it. Check the seasoning, and discard the bouquet garni. Slice the beef and return it to the casserole. Serve very hot, in the pot, with fettuccini noodles.

When the meat is soft, you can add 2 tablespoons wine vinegar to strengthen the flavor.

All slow-cooked stews taste better reheated! You can remove the meat and refrigerate it for 12 hours, then slice it cold and return it to the casserole with its cooking liquid. Reheat it for 30 minutes on low heat—225°F.

A contemporary note:
Before serving, sprinkle the meat with mini-croutons (1/4 inch square) that have been sautéed in butter, then add chopped parsley and tarragon and finish with button mushrooms that have been sliced in half and cooked with very tiny pieces of sautéed bacon or pork belly. Cover and reheated for 2 minutes, then serve.

Advice from the wine steward:
Accompany this beef stew with a red wine such as a Margaux.

Pork Belly
with Buttered Cabbage

Preparation time: 30 min.
Cooking time: 4 hrs. total, divided into two

To serve 6

2 lb 12oz	lightly salted pork belly or pancetta
2	carrots
2	celery stalks
1	bouquet garni
4	onions
2	cloves
2	large savoy cabbages
5½ oz	smoked pork belly
6 tbsp	butter
	salt and pepper

1. If using pork belly, put it into a Le Creuset French oven. Cover it with cold water, bring it gently to the boil, and boil for 2–3 minutes, skimming the surface. Drain the pork belly, rinse it under cold running water, and drain it.

2. Peel the carrots and wash them with the celery stalks and the bouquet garni. Peel 2 of the onions and stick a clove in each.

3. Put the meat into a Le Creuset French oven and cover it with cold water again. Bring it slowly to the boil and skim the surface. Add the carrots, the 2 onions with the cloves, the celery, and bouquet garni. Cover and simmer for 3 hours with the water just shivering.

4. Drain the meat and strain the cooking liquid. Leave it to cool, then refrigerate both the meat and the liquid.

5. The next day, trim the cabbages and discard the outer leaves. Cut out the thickest ribs from the leaves. Boil a large pot of water, season it with salt, throw the cabbage leaves into it, and boil for 3 minutes. Drain them and rinse them under cold water to refresh them. Drain them again carefully.

6. Preheat the oven to 425°F. Cut off the rind, fat and cartilage of the smoked pork belly and cut it into short strips. Peel the remaining 2 onions and mince them. Melt the butter in a Le Creuset round pot, add the onions and strips of smoked pork, and cook on low heat for 10 minutes. The smoked pork should not color.

7. Add the cabbage with 2 cups of the cooking liquid from the salt pork belly. Cover with the lid, place in the oven, and bake for 40 minutes.

8. Remove from the oven and leave to cool. Heat a nonstick skillet and sauté the meat on medium heat until it is lightly browned all over. Place the meat on top of the cabbage, in the saucepan but do not cover it. Return it to the oven and cook for another 10 minutes. Season with pepper and serve very hot.

Advice from the wine steward:
Accompany the pork belly with a red wines such as a Saint-Joseph.

Ham Hock
with Foie Gras

Soaking time: 4 hrs.
Preparation time: 30 min.
Cooking time: 6 hrs.

To serve 6-8

1	salted ham hock, about 3 lb after boning
2¼ lb	duck fat
1 lb	raw duck foie gras
	salt and pepper
4	garlic cloves
1	onion
1 tbsp	oil
⅓ cup	wine vinegar
3	sprigs of thyme
1	sprig of rosemary

1. Put the salted ham hock into a large bowl of cold water to remove the salt and soak for 4 hours in frequent changes of water. .

2. Melt the duck fat on low heat in a Le Creuset oval French oven.

3. Heat the oven to 200°F. Cut the foie gras in half. Put it in the fat, cover the pot, place it in the oven and leave it for 20 minutes. Remove it from the pot, reserving the fat, and leave it to cool to room temperature.

4. Drain the ham hock, rinse it, pat it dry, and add it to the duck fat. Cover the pot and return it to the oven. Cook very gently in the oven for 5 hours.

5. Using a small, pointed knife, cut the nerves out of the foie gras. Dice the foie gras and season it with salt and pepper.

6. Peel the garlic cloves. Cook the garlic on a very low heat in a heavy-based saucepan for 15 minutes. Peel the onion and slice it thinly. Heat the oil in a small skillet and sauté the onion just until it is transparent. Then add the vinegar and scrape the bottom of the skillet with a wooden spatula to dislodge any bits sticking to it. Leave the liquid to evaporate then remove from the heat. Remove the leaves from the thyme and rosemary sprigs and grind them in a food processor.

7. Drain the ham hock and leave to cool. Remove the rind and any fat that needs removing. Shred the meat. Slice the cooked garlic into strips. Combine the meat with the foie gras, onion, slices of garlic, thyme, and rosemary. Season with salt and pepper. Press the mixture into a single lump and place it in a 2½-quart Le Creuset oval pot. Cover with the lid, place the pot in a bain-marie of hot water and cook in a 250°F oven for 30 minutes.

8. Remove from the oven and leave to cool to room temperature.

Served with a potato salad, the shredded ham hock makes an excellent summer dish. You can also serve it as an appetizer with toasted whole-wheat bread.

Prepared in this way, the ham hock can be kept for up to seven days in the refrigerator.

Advice from the wine steward:
Accompany the ham hock with a red wine such as a Madiran.

Pork Cheek
with Lentils

Preparation time: 30 min.
Cooking time: 2 hrs. 30 min.

To serve 4

3	carrots
3	onions
8	pork cheeks
	salt and pepper
	flour
2 tbsp	oil
4½ tbsp	butter
1 tbsp	tomato paste
2	bouquets garnis
1 cup	dry white wine
2 quarts	chicken broth
3½ oz	smoked pork belly
1¾ cups	lentils

1. Peel, wash, and dice the carrots. Peel the onions and chop them. Season the pork cheeks with salt and pepper, then dust them with the flour. Heat the oven to 300°F.

2. Heat the oil in a Le Creuset round pot. On medium heat, sauté the pork cheeks until they turn color. Remove them from the heat and degrease the pot.

3. Melt 2 tablespoons of the butter in the round pot, then add two-thirds of the carrots and onions. Leave to cook on low heat for 3 minutes, then add the tomato paste and 1 bouquet garni. Sprinkle with the white wine. Stir the bottom of the pot with a wooden spatula to dislodge any bits that have stuck and bring the liquid to the boil.

4. Return the pork cheeks to the pot. Add 1 quart chicken broth and bring to the boil. Cover the pot and place it in the oven. Leave it to cook for two and a half hours.

5. 1 hour before serving, Remove the rind and cartilage from the smoked pork belly and cut it into short strips. Heat the rest of the butter in a Le Creuset heavy-based saucepan or Le Creuset French oven. Add the pieces of smoked pork belly and the rest of the carrots and onions. Cook on low heat for 3 minutes. Add the lentils, the other bouquet garni, and 1 quart chicken broth. Bring slowly to the boil, cover, and cook on a low boil for around 35 minutes, or until the lentils are soft. Season the lentils lightly with salt when they are three-quarters through the cooking time. Add a little liquid during cooking if the lentils have absorbed all the original liquid.

6. Discard the bouquet garni from the pork cheeks and lentils. Drain the lentils and serve with the cheeks and their cooking liquid. Serve the dish piping hot.

Advice from the wine steward:
Accompany the pork cheeks with a red wine such as a Pessac-Léognan.

Roast Pork
with Prune Stuffing

Preparation time: **25 min.**
Cooking time: **2 hrs.**

To serve 6

12	large prunes
2 lb 12 oz	pork fillet, boned and rolled
2	carrots
1	onion
	salt and pepper
4 tsp	butter
3 tbsp	Armagnac
1	sprig of thyme
1	bay leaf
2 tbsp	heavy cream
2 tbsp	oil

1. Pit the prunes, leaving the fruits whole. Stick the spit of a roasting spit through one end of the pork fillet pushing it almost through to the other end. Remove the spit and in this hole, push the handle of a wooden spoon or a sharpening steel and gradually widen the cavity to make a tunnel. Remove the ustensily.

2. Push the prunes into this tunnel and push them down with the wooden spoon handle. Close the opening by folding a flap of the meat over it.

3. Peel the carrots and the onion. Wash the carrots, and slice them and the onion into thin rings.

4. Season the pork roast with salt and pepper. Heat it on medium heat in a Le Creuset oval pot. Add the butter and cook the roast all over until browned. Add the Armagnac and set it alight.

5. Add the carrots and the onion, and cook on low heat for a few minutes. Add ⅔ cup water, the thyme and the bay leaf. Cover and simmer on low heat for about 2 hours. Add a little hot water during the cooking if necessary.

6. Drain the meat. Strain the cooking liquid and degrease it to make a gravy. Check the seasoning and pour the gravy into a warmed sauceboat. Discard the string from the pork roast and slice it.

Advice from the wine steward:
Accompany this pork roast with a red wine such as Montagne-Saint-Emilion.

Leg of Veal
with Citrus

Preparation time: **25 min.**
Cooking time: **1 hr. 30 min.**

To serve 4

2	long, thin carrots
1	tomato
1	stick celery, with leaves
1	onion
3	sprigs of flat-leaf parsley
1	sprig of thyme
1	bay leaf
2	garlic cloves
1	untreated orange
1	untreated lemon
	salt and pepper
4	slices round leg of veal, each about 1 inch thick
	all-purpose flour
3 tbsp	olive oil
3½ tbsp	butter
1 tbsp	tomato paste
⅓ cup	dry white wine
⅓ cup	veal or chicken broth
1 tbsp	aged wine vinegar

1. Peel the carrots, wash them, and dice them. Wash and skin the tomato, discard the hard core and seeds, then chop the pulp coarsely. Cut off and reserve the celery leaves. Remove the strings and slice thinly. Peel the onion and chop it finely. Rinse the parsley, celery leaves, thyme, and bay leaf. Peel the garlic and crush the cloves

2. Brush the orange and lemon under hot water, and wipe them dry. Cut off a thin strip of peel about 1 inch long, making sure not to include white parts.

3. Salt and pepper the slices of veal leg, coat them with the flour, and shake to remove the excess.

4. Heat the olive oil in a Le Creuset oval pot on medium heat. Sauté the veal slices in the hot oil and leave them to brown. Remove them with a skimmer and place them on a plate.

5. Put 4 teaspoons butter into the pot. When it has melted, add the carrots, slices of celery, onion, and garlic. Leave for 3 minutes on low heat. Add the vinegar and scrape the bottom of the pot with a wooden spoon to remove any bits that have stuck to it.

6. Add the tomato and tomato paste. Mix well and season lightly with salt and pepper. Arrange the slices of veal on the bed of vegetables. Sprinkle with the white wine and broth, and add the herbs, tied in a bunch. Bring to the boil, cover, lower the heat, and cook for 1 hour. Season with pepper and cook for another 15 to 30 minutes, or until the meat is very tender.

7. Finely grate half the lemon and orange zest and mix them with the rest of the butter. Cut the rest of the peel into thin strips using a citrus zester. Add them to a small saucepan of cold water, bring to the boil, drain, and rinse them in cold water.

8. Discard the bunch of herbs and strips of peel from the saucepan. Add the lemon-and-orange-flavored butter. Mix lightly and leave to simmer for few minutes more. Garnish the slices of veal with the strips of peel. Serve very hot.

Advice from the wine steward:
Accompany this leg of veal with a red wine such as Châteauneuf-du-Pape.

Blanquette of Veal
in Traditional Style

Preparation time: 30 min.
Cooking time: 1 hr. 30 min.

To serve 4

1 lb 2 oz	breast of veal with bones
1 lb 2 oz	shoulder of veal
1	carrot
1	leek
1	small celery stick
1	bay leaf
2	sprigs of flat-leaf parsley
1	onion
1 tbsp	oil
3 tbsp	butter
	salt and pepper
1 tbsp	all-purpose flour
4	black peppercorns
	coarse salt
2 cups	button mushrooms
1	lemon juice
12	pearl onions
½ tsp	sugar
2	egg yolks
⅓ cup	heavy cream
1	clove

1. Cut the breast and shoulder into equal bite-sized pieces if the butcher has not already done so.

2. Peel the carrot and leek and wash them. Slice the carrot into rounds and slice the leek into thin strips. Remove the strings from the celery stick and slice it. Tie the green part of the leek with the bay leaf and parsley into a bunch. Peel the onion and stick a clove into it.

3. Heat the oil and 4 teaspoons butter on medium heat in a Le Creuset French oven. Add the meat and sauté it on low-to-medium heat, without letting it brown. Season with salt and pepper. Sprinkle with flour, mix well with a wooden spoon and cook for 1 minute.

4. Barely cover with hot water and bring slowly to the boil. skim the surface. Add the carrot, leek, bunch of herbs, onion, and peppercorns. Season with the coarse salt. Cover the pot with a lid and cook for 1 hour to 1 hour 15 minutes, at a slow boil, until the meat is tender.

5. During the cooking, trim the mushroom stalks and rinse them but do not soak them. Put them into a saucepan with 2 teaspoons butter and 1 teaspoon lemon juice. Cover with boiling water, season with salt, and cook for 10 minutes. Drain them, retaining the cooking liquid.

6. Peel the pearl onions, put them into a small saucepan, cover them with water, add 2 teaspoons butter, and the sugar. Cover with a disk of nonstick baking paper and cook until the liquid has completely evaporated. Coat the onions in the glaze.

7. Remove the meat from the pot and filter the cooking liquid through a fine sieve. Pour it into the saucepan and reduce it to 2 cups. Add the mushroom cooking liquid. Combine the egg yolks and cream in a bowl and beat with a whisk. Beat in 1 tablespoon of lemon juice. Pour a ladleful of soup into the bowl, beating constantly. Pour the liquid into the pot, continuing to beat with a whisk. Bring just to the boil, beating constantly.

8. Check the seasoning. Add the meat to the sauce and reheat for a few minutes on a low heat. Add the mushrooms and pearl onions. Serve hot from the pot.

Advice from the wine steward:
Accompany this veal blanquette with a red wine, such as Hautes-Côtes-de-Nuits.

Casserole of Veal
Fillet

Preparation time: 30 min.
Cooking time: 2 hrs.

To serve 6

2½ lb	fillet (leg round) of veal
	salt and pepper
2	garlic cloves
3 tbsp	olive oil
4 tbsp	sweet white wine
3	sprigs of thyme
⅓ cup	chicken broth
2	bunches baby carrots with their tops
30	pearl onions
3 tbsp	butter
1 tsp	sugar

1. Season the veal fillet with salt and pepper. Peel the garlic cloves and crush them. Let the broth cool.

2. Heat the oil in a Le Creuset Doufeu pot. Add 4 teaspoons of butter. Brown the meat all over on medium heat. Add the wine and scrape the bottom of the pot with a wooden spatula to dislodge any bits that have stuck to it. Add the garlic and the thyme. Add the broth, cover the pot, and pour iced water into the concave lid. Simmer on very low heat.

3. Scrape the carrots, leaving just under an inch of tops. Wash them and add them to the pot when the contents have been cooking for 1 hour and 15 minutes. Cook for another 45 minutes. Pour more iced water into the lid if it has evaporated.

4. Peel the pearl onions and put them into a small saucepan with 4 teaspoons butter, the sugar, and 3 tablespoons water. Cover with a disk of nonstick baking paper and cook the onions for ten minutes or so. Then coat them with the glaze that has formed. Add the meat 10 minutes before the end of the cooking time.

5. Drain the meat and vegetables and discard the thyme. Degrease the cooking liquid and pour it into a warmed sauceboat to serve as gravy.

Advice from the wine steward:
Accompany this fillet of veal with a red wine such as a Saint-Chinian.

Poultry

Produce: choices and advice

Poultry

Squab:
In France, a squab is less than 28 days old. After that, it becomes a pigeon, whose flesh is much firmer. If squab is not available, substitute rock Cornish hen. The birds should be plump, with well rounded breasts, and firm to the touch.

Garden peas:
Choose small peas with firm, bright green, smooth and shiny pods.

Rooster (stewing hen):
Always buy a young bird that is not too fatty, weighing between 4½ and 6½ lb. If it is heavier, and thus older, it is liable to be tough.It should be cooked very slowly and will taste best if reheated.

Chicken:
Whether the skin is yellow or white, a good chicken has a supple wishbone and a thin layer of fat on the back.

Chicken broth:
See page 10.

Hen:
This is a young, fairly lean, chicken weighing about 4½ lb. Ask the butcher to gut and truss it and remove the wishbone, to make it easier to carve after cooking. Remove the fat on the inside, around the crop, before cooking.
Thoroughly clean the giblets (neck, wingtips, liver, and gizzard).

Duckling:
Canvasback ducks are the finest in the United States. The ducks are more fleshy and tender than the drakes. If you are sold a drake, be sure to remove the large sebaceous gland near the crop which will otherwise give the flesh a musky smell.

Rabbit:
See page 10.

Mustard:
Use a strong, white Dijon mustard, though don't go as far as buying the extra-strong version. Wholegrain mustard is mustard that contains some crushed mustard seed.

Roast Squab
with Garden Peas

Preparation time: 30 min.
Cooking time: 40 min.

To serve 4

4	squab, gutted and trussed, neck and giblets reserved
2	shallots
2	garlic cloves
1 tbsp	oil
	salt and pepper
½ cup	butter
4lb 8 oz	fresh garden peas, in the pod
1	onion
2	carrots
3 tbsp	wine vinegar
1 cup	chicken broth

1. Heat the oven to 475°F. Clean the squab livers and gizzards. Peel and chop the shallots. Peel and crush the garlic. Pour 1 tablespoon oil into a Le Creuset pot. Add all the giblets, the shallots, and garlic. Season the squab with salt and pepper. Place them in the pot and brush each with 2 teaspoons butter. Roast in the oven for 20 minutes.

2. Shell the peas. Peel and mince the onion. Peel the carrots and cut them into rounds. Melt 3½ tablespoons butter in a Le Creuset Doufeu oven. Sauté the onion and carrots, but do not let them brown. Add the peas, and leave to cook for 2 minutes on low heat. Add 1 scant cup boiling water and season with salt. Cover the pot. Pour ice-cold water into the concave lid of the Doufeu pot and simmer for around 8 minutes. Check the cooking which may vary depending on the quality of the peas.

3. As soon as the peas are cooked, drain them, and return them to the Doufeu pot with a few tablespoons of their cooking liquid. Then add 4 teaspoons butter.

4. When the squab have been cooking for 20 minutes, remove them from the oven and add them to the peas. Sprinkle with freshly ground black pepper. Cover the Doufeu pot.

5. Degrease the squab cooking liquid. Add the vinegar to the saucepan and scrape the bottom of the pot with a wooden spatula to dislodge any bits that have stuck to it. Add the chicken broth and simmer for 15 minutes.

6. Strain the cooking liquid and lightly coat the squab with a little of it. Pour the rest into a heated sauceboat and bring to the table with the pot containing the squab.

Advice from the wine steward:
Accompany the squab with a red wine such as Saint-Estèphe.

Coq au vin

Preparation time: **1 hr.**
Marinating time: **24 hrs.**
Cooking time: **2 hrs. 15 min.**

To serve 6

	For the marinade:
1	carrot
2	onions
2	shallots
2	garlic cloves
1	sprig of thyme
1	bayleaf
1	celery stick
5	parsley roots
1 tsp	peppercorns
6 cups	red Burgundy

1 rooster	or boiling hen, weighing 5lb 8 oz to 6 lb, gutted and cut into serving pieces
3 tbsp.	oil
5 tbsp	butter
3 tbsp.	cognac
	salt
2 cups	small cultivated mushrooms
8 oz	salted pork belly
1 cup	pearl onions
1 tsp	sugar

Advice from the wine steward:
Accompany the Coq au Vin with a red wine such as a Pomerol.

1. To make the marinade, peel the carrot, onions, and shallots and slice them into rounds. Peel and crush the garlic cloves. Put these ingredients into a Le Creuset pot with the thyme, bayleaf, celery, parsley roots, and peppercorns. Add the red wine. Add the roaster, cover the pot, and leave to marinate in the refrigerator for 24 hours.

2. When the roaster has finished marinating, drain it and pat it dry with kitchen paper. Strain the marinade and reserve the herbs and vegetables from it.

3. Heat the oil in a Le Creuset casserole. Add 2 tablespoons butter and when it foams, add the chicken pieces and brown them all over. Remove them with a skimmer and arrange them on a dish.

4. Heat the marinade in a saucepan. Preheat the oven to 375°F.

5. Add the vegetables and spices from the marinade to the casserole and cook for 3 minutes on low heat. Remove them with a skimmer and discard any grease in the casserole. Return the vegetables to the casserole. Arrange the pieces of chicken on top and reheat for 1 minute. Heat the cognac in a ladle, pour it over the chicken, and set it alight.

6. Add the boiling marinade to the casserole and simmer for 10 minutes just below the boil. Add boiling water to barely cover the chicken. Skim the surface and season with salt. Cover the casserole and put it in the oven. Leave to cook for 2 hours.

7. Trim the mushroom stalks, wash the mushrooms quickly and pat them dry. Cut the pork belly into short strips and put them into a saucepan of cold water. Bring to the boil, drain them, and rinse under cold water. Heat a skillet and brown them quickly without additional fat. Remove them from the pan. Cook the mushrooms in th same skillet with 4 teaspoons butter. Season the mushrooms.

8. Peel the pearl onions and put them into a saucepan. Barely cover them with water and add 4 teaspoons butter and the sugar. Place a disk of nonstick baking paper over the pearl onions and cook them until they are covered with a golden glaze.

9. Drain the chicken pieces. Degrease the cooking liquid and strain it. Replace the chicken in the casserole, pour the cooking liquid over it and add the pork belly, mushrooms, and onions. Leave to simmer for around 10 minutes on very low heat. Bring the casserole to the table to serve the chicken very hot on heated plates.

If you have any of the chicken blood, add 2 teaspoons wine vinegar to it and refrigerate it. Use it to thicken the gravy at the last moment.

Free-range Chicken
with Cream

Preparation time: 20 min.
Cooking time: 2 hrs.

To serve 4-5

1	oven-ready free-range chicken weighing 3lb 5oz, giblets reserved
1	large onion
1	clove
1	leek
1	carrot
1	celery stick
1	sprig of thyme
1	bay leaf
10	black peppercorns
4 tbsp	butter
3 tbsp	all-purpose flour
1¼ cups	heavy cream
2	egg yolks
	coarse salt
	salt and pepper

1. Place the chicken pieces in a Le Creuset oval French oven with the giblets around it. Add cold water to barely cover. Bring to the boil on low heat, skim the surface, then drain the chicken and rinse it under cold water.

2. Peel the onion and spike it with the clove. Peel and wash the leek and carrot and split them in half. Rinse the celery.

3. Rinse the Le Creuset pot, return the chicken and giblets to it, and add the onion, leek, carrot, celery, thyme, bay leaf, and peppercorns. Season with coarse salt. Bring gently to the boil, skim the surface, cover the pot and cook very gently for 1 hour 45 minutes.

4. Heat the butter in a saucepan, add the flour and stir for 1 minute without letting the mixture color. Leave to cool.

5. Remove 1¼ cups of the chicken cooking liquid, strain it, and degrease it. Add it to the butter-and-flour mixture and beat until the liquid returns to the boil. Cook on low heat for 10 minutes. Add the cream and simmer just below the boil for 5 minutes. Check the seasoning. Beat the egg yolks in a bowl and pour a few tablespoons of the cooking liquid into the bowl, beating constantly with a hand whisk. Pour the mixture into the pot, still beating, and cook for 1 minute while stirring, but do not let it come to the boil.

6. Drain the chicken, discarding the skin. Coat it with some of the cooking liquid and serve the rest in a heated sauceboat as a sauce.

Advice from the wine steward:
Accompany the creamed chicken with a red wine such as a Savigny-lès-Beaune.

Chicken Fricassee
with Wine Vinegar

Preparation time: 25 min.
Cooking time: 1 hr.

To serve 4-5

1	3lb 5 oz free-range chicken, cut into serving pieces
	salt
1	sprig of thyme
½	bay leaf
3	sprigs of flat-leaf parsley
1	sprig of tarragon
2	garlic cloves
2 tbsp	oil
3 tbsp	butter
1 cup	aged wine vinegar
⅓ cup	dry white wine
2 tbsp	tomato paste
	pepper
1¾ cups	chicken broth

1. Season the chicken pieces with salt. Tie the thyme, bay leaf, parsley, and tarragon together with string. Peel the garlic cloves, discarding the shoot in the center, and crush them.

2. Heat 2 tablespoons oil in a Le Creuset pot. Brown the pieces of chicken all over on medium heat. Add the butter and continue cooking, basting constantly with the butter.

3. Remove the chicken from the pot and discard the fat. Return the chicken to the pot and pour in one third of the wine vinegar. Stir with a wooden spatula to dislodge any bits that have stuck to the bottom of the pot and turn each piece over in the cooking juices that have formed, cooking until the liquid has evaporated. Do this twice more, adding the vinegar.

4. Heat the white wine with the chicken broth in a saucepan. Dilute the tomato paste with this liquid and pour it into the Le Creuset pot. Add the bunch of herbs and the garlic and bring to the boil. Cover and simmer on low heat for 1 hour.

5. Drain the chicken pieces when they are cooked and keep them warm in a shallow bowl. Bring the liquid back to the boil and check the seasoning. Strain the liquid over the fricasseed chicken. Grind pepper from a mill over the dish and serve it.

Choose a Le Creuset round or oval pot or French oven that is just large enough to hold the chicken pieces tightly together.

Advice from the wine steward:
Accompany the fricassee with a red wine, such as a Vacqueyras.

Duck

with Olives

Preparation time: 30 min.
Cooking time: 1 hr.

To serve 4

1	oven-ready duck, giblets reserved
	salt and pepper
3 tbsp	oil
100 g	lean smoked pork belly
1	carrot
1	celery stalk
1	onion
4 tsp	butter
5 tbsp	port wine
⅓ cup	chicken broth
1	sprig of thyme
1	bay leaf
100 g	black Greek olives

1. Season the outside and inside of the duck with salt and pepper. Place the liver inside it. Heat the oil in a Le Creuset oval pot. Fry the duck all over on medium heat.

2. Meanwhile, cut the pork belly into short strips. Scrape and dice the carrot. Remove the strings from the celery and slice it. Peel and chop the onion.

3. As soon as the duck is browned all over, drain it. Throw away the fat in the pot. Add the butter and melt it then add the pork belly, and the duck's neck and gizzard, the carrot, celery, and onion. Cook on medium heat, stirring constantly.

4. Add the port and scrape the bottom of the saucepan with a wooden spatula to dislodge any bits that have stuck to it. Add the chicken broth and stir again. Season with salt and pepper and add the thyme and bay leaf. Return the duck to the pot, cover it, and cook on medium heat for 50 minutes.

5. Pit the olives and add them to the duck 15 minutes before the end of the cooking time.

6. Drain the duck, carve it into serving pieces, arrange it on a warmed platter and surround it with the olives. Keep it warm. Strain the cooking liquid and degrease it, then pour it into a warmed sauceboat and serve immediately.

Advice from the wine steward:
Accompany the duck with a red wine such as Baux-de-Provence.

Rabbit

with Two Mustards

Preparation time: 35 min.
Cooking time: 1 hr.

To serve 6

3½ cups	button mushrooms
3	shallots
1	rabbit, weighing 3lb 5 oz, cut into serving pieces
	salt and pepper
3-4 tbsp	all-purpose flour
3 tbsp	oil
4 tsp	butter
⅓ cup	dry white wine
1 quart	chicken broth
1 cup	light cream
2 tbsp	strong mustard
1 tbsp	old-fashioned mustard

1. Trim the stems from the mushrooms, wash them, and slice them into four. Peel and chop the shallots.

2. Season the rabbit pieces with salt and pepper and dip them in flour, tapping them to remove any excess. Heat 2 tablespoons of oil and 4 teaspoons of butter in a Le Creuset oval pot. Brown the rabbit all over. When the pieces are nicely colored, remove them with a skimmer, and discard the grease in the pot.

3. Heat the oven to 425°F. Put 1 tablespoon oil into the pot and when it is hot, sauté the shallots and the mushrooms. Add the wine and scrape the bottom of the pot with a wooden spatula to dislodge any pieces that have stuck to it.

4. When the wine comes to the boil, put the rabbit pieces back into the pot and cover with chicken broth. Bring to the boil. Cover with the lid and put the pot into the oven. Cook for 45 minutes.

5. When the rabbit is done, remove it from the pot and arrange it on a heated serving platter. Remove the mushrooms as well and reserve them. Pour the cream into the pot and cook on the stovetop until it boils gently, then cook for another 7 or 8 minutes. Add the strong mustard, beating with a hand-whisk then add the old-fashioned mustard. Check the seasoning, strain the sauce over the rabbit and mushrooms and serve very hot.

Serve the rabbit with fresh pasta or steamed potatoes.

Advice from the wine steward:
Accompany the rabbit with a red wine such as a Côte-Rôtie.

Vegetables

Produce: choices and advice
Vegetables

Rice:
To make risotto, you need a round – or short-grained rice. The best-known varieties are Arborio and Carnarolli. These can be found in gourmet food stores. California rice can also be used.

Parmegiano reggiano:
Never buy it ready grated. Choose a nice piece of Reggiano and only grate it when you need to use it.

Ceps:
Ceps or cèpes, also known as porcini, are wild mushrooms. When buying them fresh, choose the small cork-shaped ones and make sure they are firm. Never wash them, scrape or trim the tip of the stem that is covered in earth and wipe the ceps with a damp cloth or soft, damp mushroom brush.

Chicken broth:
See page 10.

Asparagus:
The asparagus season is short, and the stalks should be very fresh. For French dishes use blanched asparagus with a pale tip and juicy stem.

Baby fennel:
These bulbs are sold in bunches. The leaves are often trimmed off before the bulb is sold.

Potatoes:
To make a gratin, choose smallish, waxy potatoes, as opposed to floury ones.

Swiss chard:
These large green leaves with thick white ribs are also called chard or silverbeet by some people. It is best to choose small leaves if you can find them. Carefully remove the transparent shiny skin that covers the ribs before use.

Pumpkin:
To reduce the cooking time, try and find a firm-fleshed yellow pumpkin weighing 3lb 5oz to 4lb 8 oz.

Tomato:
Tomatoes are seasonal and are only at their best from June through September, when they have the most flavor. Never store them in the refrigerator which will alter them, keep them at room temperature until you are ready to use them.

Eggplant:
Whether white streaked with purple, purple, or almost black, and whatever their shape, the skin must be taught and shiny and the flesh firm.

Bell peppers:
Green bell peppers are red bell peppers picked before they are ripe. Green bell peppers are very fruity and have more of a bitter taste. The skin should be smooth and shiny.

Zucchini:
Choose long ones that are not too fat and very firm to the touch.

Cabbage:
See page 50.

Polenta:
This is just the Italian name for cornmeal. Choose medium, yellow cornmeal rather than fine cornmeal. Polenta can also be sold pre-cooked or as partially cooked grits.

Globe artichokes:
The best are the small violet-tinged artichokes. All should be young, plump, and tender. Plunge them into acidulated water as soon as they are cut, to prevent them blackening in contact with the air.

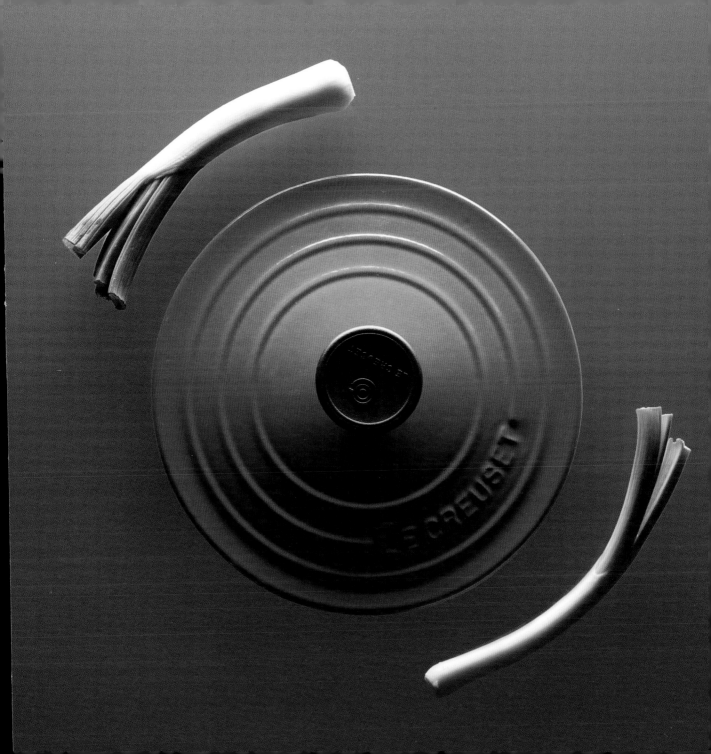

Wild Mushroom
Risotto

Preparation time: **30 min.**
Cooking time: **30 min.**

To serve 4

2 cups	ceps (porcini)
1	garlic clove
3	sprigs flat-leaf parsley
6 tbsp	Parmegiano reggiano
⅓ cup	dry white wine
2 cups	chicken broth
1 tbsp	olive oil
	salt
1	onion
6 tbsp	butter
1 cup	short-grained rice

1. Separate the stems and caps of the mushrooms. Wipe the caps with a damp cloth. Scrape the stems, rinse quickly under running water, and pat them dry with absorbent paper. Dice the stems and caps.

2. Peel and mince the garlic. Rinse the parsley, drain it, and chop the leaves. Finely grate the Parmesan cheese. Heat the broth.

3. Heat 1 tablespoon olive oil in a skillet, add the diced mushrooms, season them with salt, and sauté for 3 minutes. Drain them through a sieve, retaining the cooking juices.

4. Peel and mince the onion. Melt 2 tablespoons butter in a shallow Le Creuset pot. Cook the onion for 2 minutes without it coloring. Add the rice and stir for 2 minutes with a wooden spatula. Add the white wine and bring to the boil, stirring gently. When the liquid has been totally absorbed, add enough very hot broth to almost cover the rice. Leave it to evaporate, still stirring, adding broth and continuing to do so until the rice is cooked but al dente. Season lightly with salt.

5. Reduce the heat. Add the mushrooms, garlic, parsley, and mushroom cooking liquid to the rice and stir well. Then incorporate the Parmesan cheese and the rest of the butter, stirring lightly. Serve immediately.

When serving, you can sprinkle the risotto with a little olive oil and grind pepper over it from a peppermill.

Advice from the wine steward:
Accompany the risotto with a white wine such as a Meursault.

Spring Vegetable
Casserole

Preparation time: 30 min.
Cooking time: 30 min.

To serve 4

8	asparagus tips
8	small new turnips with their tops
12	baby carrots with their tops
8	small waxy potatoes
4	miniature fennel bulbs
4	baby zucchini
	salt
3 tbsp	olive oil
⅔ cup	chicken broth
2 tsp	butter
1 tbsp	sherry vinegar

1. Trim the ends of the stems of the asparagus. Peel the turnips and carrots, leaving ½ inch of the tops attached. Peel the potatoes. Trim off the tops and tough base of the miniature fennel bulbs. Top and tail the baby zucchini. Wash all the vegetables.

2. Bring a large pan of salted water to the boil. Add the asparagus tips and cook for 2 minutes. Drain them and rinse under cold water. Drain them again.

3. Heat 2 tablespoons olive oil in a Le Creuset Doufeu oven. Add the turnips, carrots, potatoes, fennel bulbs, and baby zucchini. Add the chicken broth and bring to the boil. Cover the pot and pour iced water into the concave lid. Cook for 15 minutes.

4. Add the asparagus tips. Cut the butter into cubes and add it. Cover again with the lid and cook on low heat for 5 minutes. If there is still liquid in the pot, remove the lid so that it can evaporate, then gently shake the pot so as to ensure that the vegetables are coated with the cooking liquid.

5. Add the vinegar, toss lightly, check the seasoning, and sprinkle the vegetables with a little olive oil.

If you do not have a Doufeu oven, gradually pour a little of the hot chicken broth over the vegetables, waiting each time for the liquid to evaporate.

Advice from the wine steward:
Accompany this vegetable casserole with a white wine, such as a Pouilly-Fumé.

Fall Vegetable
Casserole

Preparation time: 30 min.
Cooking time: 40 min.

To serve 4

1 cup	chestnuts
1	bunch pearl onions
4	carrots
4	medium potatoes
3	garlic cloves
2	very small apples
2	very small pears
3½ oz	smoked pork belly
¼	chicken bouillon cube
4 tsp	butter
	salt
2 cups	ceps
16	seedless grapes
1 tbsp	olive oil

1. Cut through the outer and inner skins of the chestnuts all around them from top to bottom. Cover the chestnuts with cold water, bring to the boil, and cook for 5 minutes. Drain the chestnuts in batches of four, passing them under the cold faucet and peeling them as they drain, while they are still hot.

2. Peel the pearl onions. Scrape the carrots, wash them, cut them into ½-inch thick rounds on the diagonal. Peel the potatoes, wash them and dice them. Peel the garlic and crush the cloves. Peel the apples and pears, cut them in half and cut out the cores.

3. Remove the rind, fat and cartilage from the pork belly, and cut it into short strips. Boil ⅓ cup water and dissolve the bouillon cube in it.

4. Melt the butter in a Le Creuset Doufeu French oven. Arrange the halved apples and pears in the bottom of the pot and roast on one side for 5 minutes, on one side only. Add the pork belly, carrots, potatoes, chestnuts, and the garlic. Sauté on medium heat for a few minutes, stirring with a wooden spatula. Season with salt and add the chicken broth. Cover the pot and pour ice cold water into the concave lid. Reduce the heat and cook for around 30 minutes.

5. Clean the ceps, by trimming the stems. Wipe the caps with damp kitchen paper. Slice the mushrooms fairly thinly. Heat 1 tablespoon olive oil in a skillet and sauté them quickly. Season with salt.

6. After they have been cooking for 30 minutes, check the seasoning for the vegetables, mix them delicately and increase the heat if necessary to enable any cooking liquid to evaporate. Add the ceps to the pot. Cover and cook for another 5 minutes.

7. Wash the grapes and add them to the pot. Replace the lid, remove from the heat, and leave to rest for 2 minutes. Toss all the vegetables in the cooking juices and bring the pot to the table.

Advice from the wine steward:
Accompany this vegetable casserole with a white wine such as Hautes-Côtes-de-Beaune.

Greek-style
Vegetables

Preparation time: 30 min.
Cooking time: 50 min.

To serve 4

2	celery sticks
1	sprig of thyme
1	bay leaf
2	parsley roots
2	garlic cloves
½	fennel bulb
4 tbsp	olive oil
1 cup	dry white wine
1 tsp	coriander seeds
5	black peppercorns
4	tiny fennel bulbs
12	small pearl onions
4	baby carrots
8 oz	zucchini
12	button mushrooms
1	lemon
2	baby violet artichokes
	salt

1. Tie the celery sticks, thyme, bay leaf, and parsley roots together. Peel the garlic cloves, cut them in half and discard the green shoot in the center. Cut the half fennel bulb into slices.

2. Heat 2 tablespoons olive oil in a shallow Le Creuset pan. Add the fennel and cook for 5 minutes, then add the white wine and scrape the bottom of the pot with a wooden spatula. Add 1 tablespoon oil and 2 cups water. Add the coriander seeds, peppercorns, and the bunch of herbs. Bring to the boil, skim, and simmer gently for 30 minutes.

3. Trim the tops and tough bases from the baby fennel bulbs. Peel the pearl onions. Peel the carrots and slice them into even rounds about ¾ inch long. Wash the zucchini and slice them to the same size as the carrots. Trim the mushroom stems and clean the mushrooms quickly. Sprinkle them with lemon juice.

4. Discard the tough outer leaves of the artichokes. Cut off the stems 1 inch from the bottoms and cut away the tough tips of the remaining leaves. Peel the stems. Cut the artichokes in half, and remove the choke if there is one. Plunge the artichokes into cold water, adding a little lemon juice to prevent discoloration.

5. Strain the contents of the pan. Heat 1 tablespoon oil in the pan and add the prepared vegetables. Season with salt. Cover and leave to cook slowly for 3 minutes. Pour the flavored broth in until it almost covers the vegetables. Cover and simmer for 10 minutes on low heat. Add the juice of ½ a lemon and sprinkle with a little olive oil. Leave to cool.

Greek-style vegetables are served very cold, but you could also serve them hot as an accompaniment or garnish for meat or fish.

Advice from the wine steward:
Accompany these vegetables with a white wine such as Menetou-Salon.

Pumpkin
Gratin

Preparation time: **10 min.**
Cooking time: **about 4 hrs.**

To serve 4

2lb 4 oz	pumpkin
2	onions
5	garlic cloves
	salt
1 tbsp	olive oil
4 tsp	butter
⅔ cup	grated Parmesan cheese

1. Preheat the oven to 300°F.

2. Discard the pumpkin seeds and fibers. Peel the pumpkin and cut it into large cubes.

3. Peel the onions. Crush the garlic cloves without peeling them.

4. Put the pumpkin, onions, and garlic into a Le Creuset pot. Season with salt and sprinkle with 1 tablespoon oil. Cover the pot and put it into the oven. Reduce the oven temperature to 250°F and cook for 4 hours.

5. If the pumpkin pulp is not sufficiently dry at the end of the cooking time, place the pot on the stovetop and cook, uncovered, until the additional moisture evaporates. Discard the garlic cloves. Grind the contents of the pot in a food processor then pour it into a gratin dish.

6. Melt the butter. Sprinkle the pumpkin with Parmesan cheese, then with the melted butter, and brown it quickly under the broiler.

A contemporary note:
Decorate the pumpkin gratin with a few horn of plenty mushrooms that have been stewed for 5 minutes in a skillet with 2 teaspoons butter and 1 crushed garlic clove.

Advice from the wine steward:
Accompany this pumpkin gratin with a white wine such as Mâcon-Villages.

Swiss Chard
Gratin

Preparation time: 30 min.
Cooking time: 40 min.

To serve 4

1	bunch Swiss chard
2 tbsp	olive oil
1	chicken bouillon cube
1	garlic clove
1 tsp	lemon juice
	salt and pepper
2 tbsp	Parmesan cheese, grated
⅓ cup	light cream
3½ tbsp	Gruyère cheese, grated

1. Carefully wash the Swiss chard. Separate the ribs from the green parts. Remove the stringy parts from the ribs. As you prepare them, plunge them into cold water to which a little lemon juice has been added. Drain them. Place them in a sauté pan with 1 tablespoon olive oil, cover and leave for 5 minutes on low heat.

2. Dissolve the bouillon cube in 2 cups boiling water. Pour this over the Swiss chard ribs. Cover and simmer for 15 minutes at a low boil.

3. Remove the large veins from the green leaves. Plunge the leaves into a saucepan of salted boiling water and cook for 5 minutes. Drain the leaves. Peel the garlic and squeeze it in a garlic press. Heat 1 tablespoon olive oil in a skillet, add the green leaves and the garlic, and fry for 1 minute. Season with salt and pepper.

4. Preheat the oven to 400°F.

5. Drain the Swiss chard. Arrange the ribs in a Le Creuset gratin dish and sprinkle them with Parmesan cheese. Arrange the green leaves on top. Pour the cream over the dish, sprinkle the Gruyère cheese evenly over the dish, put it into the oven, and cook for about 20 minutes.

Advice from the wine steward:
Accompany the gratin with a white wine such as a Rully 1er Cru.

Potato

Gratin

Preparation time: 25 min.
Cooking time: 1 hr.

To serve 4-6

2lb 4 oz	waxy potatoes
2	eggs
2 pinches	nutmeg
1 cup	light cream
1¾ cups	milk
	salt and pepper
1	large garlic clove
3 tbsp	butter

1. Peel and wash the potatoes and dry them with a clean cloth. Cut them into slices about ⅛ inch thick.

2. Break the eggs into a bowl, beat them with a fork, add 2 pinches of nutmeg, the cream, and the milk. Season with salt and pepper. Mix well.

3. Heat the oven to 325°F. Peel the garlic, cut the clove in half and rub the inside of a Le Creuset gratin dish with it. Then brush it with 4 teaspoons melted butter.

4. Arrange a layer of potatoes in the dish, coat with some of the egg-and-milk mixture, then add another layer of potatoes and another layer of the egg-and-milk mixture. Continue until the potatoes are used up and finish with the egg-and-milk mixture. Cut the rest of the butter into small cubes and sprinkle the dish with it.

5. Transfer the dish to the oven and cook for 1 hour. Bring to the table in the dish.

A true Gratin Dauphinois does not contain cheese but you can easily sprinkle grated Gruyère cheese over the dish 20 minutes before the end of the cooking time.

Advice from the wine steward:
Accompany this potato gratin with a white wine such as Côtes-du-Rhône.

Ratatouille
Niçoise

Preparation time: 35 min.
Cooking time: 45 min.

To serve 4-6

2	Japanese eggplant
2	long zucchini
1	red bell pepper
1	green bell pepper
2	large ripe tomatoes
2	medium onions
⅓ cup	olive oil
	salt and pepper
2	pinches of sugar
2	sprigs of thyme
1	bay leaf
2	garlic cloves

1. Wash the eggplant, zucchini, red and green peppers, and tomatoes. Wipe them. Trim the tips of the eggplant and zucchini. Remove the stem, seeds, and white ribs of the peppers. Cut the eggplant, zucchini, and peppers in four, then cut them into diamonds.

2. Discard the hard piece beneath the stem and the core of the tomatoes, slice them into four, and slice them into strips. Peel the onions and slice them thinly.

3. Heat 3 tablespoons olive oil in a skillet and sauté the eggplant slices. Remove them and reserve them on a dish. Add a little oil to the skillet and sauté the zucchini.

4. Heat 2 tablespoons olive oil in a Le Creuset shallow pan. Sauté the onions, add the peppers and fry for 5 minutes. Arrange the eggplant and zucchini on the other vegetables. Season with salt and pepper and sprinkle with sugar. Add the thyme and bay leaf. Mix well, cover the pan and cook on low heat for 15 minutes. Then add the tomatoes and cook for another 15 minutes.

5. Peel and mince the garlic. Add it to the pan after about 30 minutes of cooking time and cook for another 15 minutes. If there is too much cooking liquid, remove the lid partially before the end of the cooking time, to let it evaporate. Serve hot or iced.

Advice from the wine steward:
Accompany the ratatouille with a white wine such as Coteaux-d'Aix-en-Provence.

Braised Stuffed
Cabbage

To serve 4

1	Savoy cabbage
⅓ cup	rice
2	onions
2	garlic cloves
3	sprigs flat-leaf parsley
1 tbsp	oil
1 cup	sausagemeat
1	egg, beaten
	salt and pepper
2 cups	vegetable broth
1	carrot
4	thin slices smoked pork belly
1	sprig of thyme
1 tbsp	butter
1 cup	thick, fresh tomato sauce

1. Bring a large pot of salted water to the boil. Remove the core and the tough outer leaves of the cabbage. Cut right around the stem very deeply to remove as much as possible of the core without detaching the leaves. Plunge the cabbage into the boiling water and boil for 15 minutes. Drain it and rinse under cold running water.

2. Cook the rice for 15 minutes in salted boiling water. Peel the onions and the garlic. Mince the onions. Rinse the parsley, pat it dry, remove the leaves and mince them.

3. Heat the oil in a sauté pan. Sauté the onions, add the sausagemeat, and mash it with a fork. Cook for around 8 minutes, stirring frequently, until there is no more liquid. Remove it from the heat and add the parsley, drained rice, then the beaten egg. Mix well and check the seasoning.

4. Heat the oven to 350°F. Heat the broth. Peel the carrot and cut it into thin rounds.

5. Pull back four or five thicknesses of the cabbage leaves and remove the heart. Place two lengths of kitchen string in a cross on the work surface. Place the cabbage on it. Replace the heart with two-thirds of the stuffing. Cover with the first layer of leaves, then cover with a little stuffing at the base of each leaf and fold the leaves back into place. Do the same with each layer, working outward from the center. Tie the cabbage up with the string.

6. Cover a 10-inch round Le Creuset pot with the slices of pork belly. Sprinkle with the thyme and rounds of carrot and place the cabbage on top. Pour the hot broth into the pot until it comes three-quarters of the way up and bring it to the boil. Melt the butter and sprinkle the cabbage with it. Cover the pot and cook in the oven for 45 minutes. Baste the cabbage with a little of the cooking juices once or twice during the cooking time.

7. When the cabbage is tender, remove it from the pot and undo the strings. Reduce the cooking juices by half, incorporate the tomato sauce and coat the cabbage with this sauce.

Advice from the wine steward:
Accompany this stuffed cabbage with a red wine such as Crozes-Hermitage.

Polenta
in the Traditional Style

Preparation time: 10 min.
Cooking time: 1 hr. 30 min.
                     or 10 min. for precooked grits

To serve 4

1 tbsp	olive oil
	coarse salt
1 cup	medium yellow cornmeal
6 tbsp	butter
5 tbsp	Parmegiano reggiano, grated
2 tbsp	heavy cream

1. Pour 1 quart water and the olive oil into a Le Creuset round pot. Add a small handful of coarse salt. Bring to the boil and remove the pot from the heat.

2. Sprinkle the cornmeal in the pot all at once. Stir vigorously with a whisk or wooden spatula. Return the pot to the heat, bring it to the boil, stirring constantly, and cook for 5 minutes, still stirring. Scoop the polenta from the sides of the pot using a spatula. Cover and let the polenta cook for 90 minutes on a very low heat, not letting it return to the boil. Stir it frequently. If you use precooked cornmeal or grits, it should be ready in around 10 minutes.

3. Cut the butter into small cubes and incorporate it into the polenta with the grated Parmegiano reggiano and the cream. Check the seasoning. Serve immediately.

Polenta is served as an accompaniment to a dish that has plenty of sauce. You can also serve it with a tomato sauce or a wild mushroom (ceps or porcini) sauce.

Advice from the wine steward:
Accompany the polenta with a white wine such as Saint-Véran.

Desserts

Soufflé with Cointreau
and Orange Salad

Preparation time: 15 min.
Cooking time: 10 min.

To serve 6

1	untreated orange
	butter and sugar for
	the ramekins
4	whole eggs
4 tbsp	sugar
2	egg whites
5 tbsp	Cointreau liqueur

1. Heat the oven to 425°F. Butter six Le Creuset enameled stoneware ramekins with a capacity of around 7 fl oz each (just under a cup). Sprinkle the insides all over with sugar.

2. Brush the orange skin in warm water, pat it dry and finely grate the zest.

3. Separate the egg whites from the yolks. Put the yolks into a bowl, add 2 tablespoons sugar and beat the mixture until it turns pale.

4. Whip the six egg whites. As the whites begins to stiffen, gradually add 2 tablespoons sugar. Continue to beat until the egg whites form stiff peaks. Fold in the grated zest.

5. Fold the egg whites into the sugared yolks, using a metal spoon and working from bottom to top, without stirring or beating, so as to ensure the whites remain stiff. Add the Cointreau to the mixture.

6. Divide the mixture among the ramekins, place in the oven and cook for 10 minutes. Serve immediately.

A contemporary note:
Serve these soufflés hot with an orange salad. Peel 3 oranges, removing any white parts and detach the segments, retaining any juice. Melt 5 teaspoons sugar and 2 tablespoons vanilla sugar with 1 cup water in a saucepan over low heat. Add the orange juice and leave to cool, then chill. Divide the orange segments between 4 sundae glasses and sprinkle them with the syrup.

Advice from the wine steward:
Accompany the soufflé with a white wine such as Coteaux-du-Layon.

Floating Islands
with Pink Pralines

Preparation time: 20 min.
Infusion time: 10 min.
Cooking time: 15 min.

To serve 6

2 cups	milk
1	vanilla bean
5	egg yolks
7 tbsp	sugar
	butter and sugar
	for the ramekins
3¼ oz	pink pralines
6	egg whites

1. Pour the milk into a saucepan. Split the vanilla bean in half. Add it to the milk, bring to the boil, then remove from the heat and leave to infuse for 10 minutes.

2. Discard the vanilla pod and reheat the milk. Beat the egg yolks in a bowl with ⅓ cup of the sugar using a hand-held whisk, until the mixture foams and becomes paler. Gradually add the hot milk to the mixture, beating constantly. Pour it into the saucepan and cook on low heat, stirring constantly with a wooden spoon, without letting it come to the boil until the mixture coats the spoon. Immediately plunge the saucepan into a pan of cold water and leave the custard to cool.

3. Heat the oven to 325°F. Prepare a water-bath, by pouring hot water into a roasting pan. Butter six Le Creuset enameled stoneware ramekins with a capacity of around 7 fl oz each (just under a cup). Sprinkle the insides with sugar, then turn them upside down to remove excess sugar. Use a rolling pin to crush the pralines.

4. Beat the egg whites into stiff peaks. When the white are still soft, gradually add 2 table-spoons of sugar, beating constantly. When the whites are stiff, gently fold in the pralines, using a metal tablespoon. Divide the mixture among the ramekins. Smooth the top and run a finger around the inner rim of the ramekin to separate it from the edge of the ramekin.

5. Place the ramekins in a hot, but not boiling, water-bath, put them into the oven and cook for 15 minutes, or until the surface is golden.

6. Place the ramekins on a rack and leave them to cool.

7. To serve, unmold the "islands" on dessert plates and surround them with the cold custard.

The custard will have a better flavor if you infuse the milk 12 hours before making the custard.

Advice from the wine steward:
Accompany these floating island with a rosé wine such as a Bugey Cerdon.

Brioche Slices
with Fruit Compote

Preparation time: 25 min.
Cooking time: 45 min.

To serve 4

2	apples
2	pears
⅓ cup	raisins
1 cup	sugar
⅓ cup	butter
1	vanilla bean
1	cinnamon stick
2 cups	milk
2	eggs, beaten
8	slices of day-old brioche

1. Peel the apples and the pears and cut them into large cubes. Rinse the raisins. Heat the oven to 275°F.

2. Pour ⅓ cup of the sugar into a round Le Creuset pot and add 2 tablespoons water. Cook until the mixture becomes a pale caramel color.

3. Stop the cooking of the caramel by adding 3½ tablespoons butter. Add the fruits and the raisins. Cut the vanilla bean in half and split the half. Scrape out the insides over the fruit. Add the halved bean and the cinnamon stick to the pot. Transfer the pot to the oven and cook for 30 minutes, or until the fruits remain whole but become meltingly soft in the center. Add a little water if this seems necessary.

4. Bring the milk to the boil with 4 teaspoons sugar and another halved vanilla pod. Leave to infuse until it is completely cold.

5. Beat the eggs with the rest of the sugar. Quickly plunge the brioche slices in the cold milk, then into the beaten egg. Melt the rest of the butter in a nonstick skillet. When it foams, add the brioche slices, and sauté them on both sides. Serve warm with the fruit compote served separately.

You can adapt the composition of the fruits to whatever is in season.

A contemporary note:
You can add slightly sweetened whipped cream or a scoop of ice cream to this dessert.

Advice from the wine steward:
Accompany the brioche slices with a white wine such as Muscat-de-Rivesaltes.

Cherry
Clafoutis

Preparation time: **15 min.**
Cooking time: **30-35 min.**

To serve 6

4	eggs
1	pinch of salt
4 tbsp	superfine sugar
2 tsp	vanilla sugar
5 tbsp	all-purpose flour
1¼ cups	whole milk
⅓ cup	light cream
2¾ cups	cherries, preferably morello
2 tbsp	granulated sugar
	butter for the dish

1. Preheat the oven to 400°F. Butter a Le Creuset 3-quart oval ovenproof dish.

2. Break the eggs into a bowl, add the salt, the superfine sugar, and vanilla sugar. Beat with a hand whisk. Gradually beat this mixture into the flour, then beat in the milk and cream. Pour the mixture into the ovenproof dish.

3. Wash the cherries, pat them dry, and remove the stalks. Sprinkle them over the contents of the dish. Place in the oven and cook for 30 to 35 minutes.

4. Sprinkle the clafoutis with granulated sugar as soon as it is removed from the oven. Serve warm, straight from the ovenproof dish.

The cherries for a clafoutis should not be pitted because the kernels of the pits give that special flavor to the dessert.

Advice from the wine steward:
Accompany the clafoutis with a cherry brandy such as Guignolet.

Crème Brûlée

Preparation time: **10 min.**
Infusion time: **15 min.**
Cooking time: **about 45 min.**
Refrigeration time: **at least 2 hrs.**

To serve 6

1¾ cups	whole milk
1 cup	light cream
2	vanilla beans
6	egg yolks
½ cup	superfine sugar
3 tbsp	soft brown sugar

1. Pour the milk and light cream into a saucepan. Split the vanilla beans in half, scrape out the seeds inside them over the saucepan, add the beans, and bring to the boil. Cover, remove from the heat, and leave to infuse for 15 minutes or until the mixture is cold.

2. Heat the oven to 210°F.

3. Beat the egg yolks and superfine sugar in a bowl, then stir with a wooden spoon until the mixture is pale and foaming. Remove the vanilla beans from the milk and pour the milk into the bowl, stirring without beating so as not to incorporate too much air.

4. Strain this custard through a fine sieve. Divide it between 6 Le Creuset fried egg dishes. Place them in the oven and cook for 45 minutes. The center of the custard should still be loose.

5. Remove the dishes from the oven and leave them to cool at room temperature. Refrigerate the cooled custards for at least two hours.

6. A few minutes before serving, pat the surface of the custards with kitchen paper. Sprinkle them generously with the brown sugar and transfer them to a preheated broiler on the highest setting to caramelize the brown sugar. Serve immediately.

Advice from the wine steward:
Accompany these crèmes brûlées with an aged dark rum.

Cream Caramel

To serve 6

7 tbsp	superfine sugar
2 tbsp	lemon juice
2 cups	whole milk
2	whole eggs
4	egg yolks
2 tbsp	vanilla sugar

1. Pour 5 tablespoons superfine sugar into a saucepan. Add 2 tablespoons cold water. Heat the sugar on a low heat, then bring to the boil and cook until the sugar turns pale brown. Stop it caramelizing further by adding the lemon juice. Immediately pour the caramel into six Le Creuset enameled stoneware ramekins with a capacity of around 7 fl oz each (just under a cup).

2. Heat the oven to 400°F. Prepare a water-bath by pouring hot water into a roasting pan.

3. Bring the milk to the boil. Break the eggs into a bowl, add the 4 yolks, the rest of the superfine sugar and the vanilla sugar. Beat until the mixture is smooth. Gradually add the boiling milk, beating constantly with a wooden spoon.

4. Strain the mixture through a fine sieve and divide it between the ramekins.

5. Place the ramekins in the water-bath, the water should be hot but not boiling. Place in the oven and cook for 30-35 minutes.

6. When the cooking is complete, insert a knife-blade into the custard—it should come out dry. Remove the ramekins from the water-bath and bain-marie and leave them to cool at room temperature. When they are cold, refrigerate them.

7. To serve, unmold the caramel custard onto dessert plates.

Advice from the wine steward:
Accompany this crème caramel with a sweet amber-colored wine such as Rivesaltes Ambré.

Spiced, Stewed Pears
with Pear Liqueur Custard

Preparation time: 10 min.
Cooking time: 20-25 min.
Refrigeration time: 24 hrs.

To serve 4

1	lemon
4	pears (Comice, Conference, etc.)
1	cardamom pod
3 cups	red Burgundy
½ cup	sugar
1	cinnamon stick
1	vanilla bean
1	strip orange peel 1 inch long
4	black peppercorns

1. Cut a strip of peel around 1 inch long from the lemon, using a small, sharp knife, ensuring you do not include any of the white part with it. Cut the lemon in half and squeeze the juice.

2. Pour water into a bowl and add the lemon juice. Wash the pears and wipe them dry. Peel them carefully, leaving the stem attached. As you peel each one, plunge it into the acidulated water to prevent oxidation. Crush the cardamom pod and reserve the seeds.

3. Put the pear peelings into a Le Creuset 8-inch diameter pot. Add the red wine, sugar, cinnamon stick, vanilla bean split in half, the lemon and orange peels, cardamom seeds, and peppercorns. Bring to the boil.

4. Drain the pears, place them in the wine, reduce the heat, cover the pot, and poach the pears with the water barely moving for 20 to 25 minutes, depending on the size of the fruits.

5. Leave the pears to cool in the cooking liquid. Then place them in a bowl and strain the cooking liquid over them. Refrigerate them and leave to macerate for 24 hours.

6. Remove the pears from the bowl with a skimmer, place each in a large sundae glass, coat with a little of the cooking liquid, and serve chilled.

A contemporary note:
Serve the pears with a thick custard made from 2 cups milk, 4 egg yolks, 6 tablespoons sugar, and 4 tablespoons flour. When the custard is cooked, flavor it with 2 tablespoons Williamine (pear liqueur), and sprinkle it with slivered almonds toasted for 10 minutes in a 350°F oven.

Advice from the wine steward:
Accompany these stewed pears with a white wine such as an Alsace-Tokay-Pinot Gris.

Upside Down Apple Tart

Preparation time: 30 min.
Resting time for the dough: 1 hr.
Cooking time: about 30 min.

To serve 6

1½ cups all-purpose flour
6 tbsp butter, at room temperature
¼ tsp salt
2 tbsp confectioner's sugar
1 egg yolk
1 cup superfine sugar
2lb 12oz Boskop or Golden Delicious apples

1. Sift the flour onto the work surface, add the softened butter, and incorporate it, mixing with the fingertips, until you have a mixture resembling breadcrumbs.

2. Make a well in the center of butter-and-flour mixture. Into it pour the salt, 1 tablespoon water, the confectioner's sugar, and egg yolk. Gradually incorporate all the ingredients in the well into the flour, beating only just until smooth so as to avoid overkneading the dough. Roll it into a ball, cover in plastic wrap, and leave in the refrigerator for 1 hour.

3. Core the apples with an apple-corer. Peel them and cut them in half.

4. Pour the superfine sugar into a Le Creuset 10-inch Tarte Tatin dish. Barely cover it with water and cook over a low heat, then bring to the boil, and continue cooking until the sugar caramelizes to a golden color. Remove it from the heat and leave to cool.

5. Heat the oven to 350°F.

6. When the caramel has set, arrange the halved apples tightly in the dish, cut sides upward. Cover with aluminum foil and place in the oven.

7. When the fruits have melted and taken on a caramel color, 15-20 minutes, remove them from the oven and leave to cool.

8. Increase the oven temperature to 400°F. Roll out the dough and cut out a 10-cm round. Push the apples closely together and cover them with the round of dough. Cut it with two or three slashes of a knife. Return the dish to the oven and bake for 15 minutes or until the pastry takes on a golden color.

9. Remove from the oven and leave to cool for 10 minutes, then place a serving dish on top of the pastry and turn ovenproof dish and serving dish upside down together to unmold the tart. Slice it into the Le Creuset Tatin dish which will keep it warm.

If the tart cools completely before you are ready to unmold it, reheat the ovenproof dish on quite a high heat for a few minutes, to soften the caramel, before unmolding it.

Advice from the wine steward:
Accompany this apple tart with a white wine such as Bonnezeaux.

Fruit Cake

Preparation time: 20 min.
Baking time: 45 min.

To serve 6-8

	butter for the dish
3 tbsp	currants
3 tbsp	yellow raisins
½ cup	mixed candied fruits (cherries, orange peel, angelica, pineapple, etc.)
½ cup	softened butter
½ cup	sugar
3	eggs
1¾ cups	all-purpose flour
1 tsp	baking powder
2	pinches of salt
2 tbsp	rum or cognac
2 tbsp	slivered almonds

1. Butter a Le Creuset cake pan. Cover the base with a disk of buttered nonstick baking paper. Heat the oven to 350°F.

2. Rinse the currants and yellow raisins and pat them dry. Chop the candied fruits into little dice.

3. In a bowl, combine the butter and sugar to obtain a creamy mixture. Beat in the eggs, one at a time, to obtain a creamy mixture. Sift the flour, baking powder, and salt into a bowl. Add them gradually to the butter and sugar mixture, beating well until you have a smooth dough. Flavor it with the rum or cognac.

4. Incorporate the raisins and candied fruits into the dough. Transfer the dough to the pan, and make a slight depression in the center with the back of a metal spoon dipped in cold water. Sprinkle with the slivered almonds.

5. Put the pan in the oven and cook for 45 minutes. Check for doneness by inserting a wooden skewer into the center of the cake. It should come out dry.

6. Leave the cake to rest for 15 minutes in the pan, before umolding it and leaving it to cool completely on the cake rack.

Advice from the wine steward:
Accompany this cake with a dessert white wine such as Muscat-de-Beaumes-de-Venise.

Apple

Crumble

Preparation time: 20 min.
Cooking time: 30 min.

To serve 6

1½ cups	all-purpose flour
⅔ cup	ground almonds
⅔ cup	brown sugar
¾ cup	butter
1lb 5 oz	apples
1	lemon
3 tbsp	granulated sugar
2 tbsp	currants
	butter for the dish
1 tsp	cinnamon

1. To make the dough, sift the flour and ground almonds into a bowl and add the brown sugar. Dice ⅔ cup butter and add it. Mix it all quickly with your fingertips until it has the consistency of breadcrumbs. Place in the refrigerator.

2. Peel and quarter the apples, core them, and sprinkle with the lemon juice. Then cut each quarter in half. Heat the rest of the butter in a skillet. Add the apples, sprinkle them with 2 tablespoons of the granulated sugar and leave them to cook on low heat for 5 to 10 minutes. Rinse the currants and mix them with the apples.

3. Heat the oven to350°F. Butter a Le Creuset 2½-quart gratin dish.

4. Arrange the apples in the dish in a single layer and sprinkle them with cinnamon. Cover with the crumble mixture, sprinkling it to separate with your fingers. Bake for 30 minutes.

Serve warm with clotted cream, whipped cream, vanilla ice cream, or caramel.

The shape of the ovenproof dish does not matter, it can be round, oval, or rectangular, this has no effect on the finish of the dessert. Choose the size on the basis of that of the fruits which need to be arranged in a single layer.

Advice from the wine steward:
Accompany the crumble with a sweet apple cider.

Chocolate Cake
with Chocolate Sauce

Preparation time :   **30 min.**
Cooking time: **40 min.**
Chilling time: **1 hr.**

To serve 6

	butter and flour for the dish
8 oz	baking chocolate with 70% cocoa mass
¾ cup	butter
5	eggs
1 cup	sugar
5 tbsp	all-purpose flour
1 cup	milk

1. Heat the oven to 325°F. Butter a Le Creuset square, 1.5 quart ovenproof dish, then dust it lightly with flour. Turn the dish over and tap it to remove excess flour.

2. Break 6 of the chocolate squares (6 ounces) into pieces and add them to a metal bowl. Add all but 1 tablespoon of the butter and leave to melt over a saucepan of simmering water. When the chocolate has melted, stir it well and remove the bowl from the water-bath.

3. Combine the eggs with the sugar, but do not mix too thoroughly. Sift the flour over the bowl and incorporate it. Combine this mixture with the melted chocolate.

4. Pour this mixture into the ovenproof dish. Bake it for 30 minutes then leave the cake to cool before unmolding it onto a cake platter.

5. To make the sauce, break the rest of the chocolate into pieces and put them in a metal bowl with the milk. Melt over a saucepan of simmering water. Mix carefully when the chocolate has melted. Cut the rest of the butter into dice and incorporate it. Pour this into a sauceboat and bring to the table to serve with the cake.

A contemporary note:
If you want a meltingly soft cake, reduce the cooking time by 5 minutes and serve it in the cake pan at room temperature.

Advice from the wine steward:
Accompany the cake with a red dessert wines such as Banyuls Rancio.

Index of Main Ingredients

Index of Recipes

Thanks are due to the Le Creuset company and especially to Florence Mairesse who made available to us all of the cookware—saucepans, terrines, French ovens, ramekins, and more—of every color and shape for the creation of this recipe book dedicated to all those who love casserole cooking!

Thanks to David Rathgeber, chef of "Aux Lyonnais", for his carefully thought out recipes created in the ideal setting of his restaurant located at 32 rue Saint-Marc, Paris, with the valuable assistance of Sebastien Guénard, helped by Pierre Fougére and Hervé Garnier, not forgetting the excellent advice of wine steward Guillem Kerambrun.

Thanks to Elisa Vergne who made all of the chef's recipes accessible with such talent and accuracy.

Thanks to Thomas Duval who photographed dishes and recipes with elegance and style to delight the eye and the tastebuds.

And thanks are due to Philippe David as art editor and to Mélanie Bourgoin for the page layout that enhances the attractive look of this book.

Series editors
Hélène Picaud and Emmanuel Jirou-Najou

Editorial secretary
Marie-Alice Chicou

Photographs
Thomas Duval

Graphic design and computer layout
Philippe David and Mélanie Bourgoin

Photographic post-production
José Lamouche

Translation
Josephine Bacon, American Pie

Printed in Singapore by KHL Co Pte Ltd
Legal deposit: July 2005
ISBN: 2-84123-099-6

Le Creuset, Cookbook© Lec, 2005
All rights reserved. No part of this book may be reproduced in any form, without written permission of the publisher.
Lec-Les Editions Culinaires
84 Avenue Victor Cresson
92441 Issy-les-Moulineaux cedex, France
tel +33 1 58 00 21 66
s.ruyer@alain-ducasse.com
www.alain-ducasse.com

Distributed in North America by
Stewart, Tabori & Chang
An imprint of Harry N. Abrams, Inc.
115 West 18th Street
New York, NY 10011
www.hnabooks.com